Psalms

for
Zero
Gravity

Psalms
for
Zero
Gravity

Prayers for Life's Emigrants

Edward Hays

Forest of Peace
Publishing

Suppliers for the Spiritual Pilgrim
Leavenworth, KS

Other Books by the Author:
(available through the publisher or your favorite bookstore)

Prayers and Rituals

Prayers for a Planetary Pilgrim
Prayers for the Domestic Church
Prayers for the Servants of God

Contemporary Spirituality

The Old Hermit's Almanac
The Lenten Labyrinth
Holy Fools & Mad Hatters
A Pilgrim's Almanac
Pray All Ways
Secular Sanctity
In Pursuit of the Great White Rabbit
The Ascent of the Mountain of God
Feathers on the Wind

Parables and Stories

The Gospel of Gabriel
The Quest for the Flaming Pearl
St. George and the Dragon
The Magic Lantern
The Ethiopian Tattoo Shop
Twelve and One-Half Keys
Sundancer
The Christmas Eve Storyteller

Psalms for Zero Gravity

copyright © 1998, by Edward M. Hays

Library of Congress Cataloging-in-Publication Data

Hays, Edward M.
    Psalms for zero gravity : prayers for life's emigrants / Edward Hays.
       p.   cm.
    Includes bibliographical references and index.
    ISBN 0-939516-42-X
    1. Prayers. 2. Meditations. 3. Christianity and other religions.
  I. Title.
  BL560.H39 1998
  291.4'33—dc21   98-39693
                                    CIP

published by
Forest of Peace Publishing, Inc.
PO Box 269
Leavenworth, KS 66048-0269   USA
1-800-659-3227

printed by
Hall Commercial Printing
Topeka, KS 66608-0007

1st printing: September 1998

The cover photo shows a U.S. space shuttle on a fog-shrouded launching pad.

Dedication

This book of contemporary psalms
is dedicated with gratitude
to

Dr. Ralph D. Sturm

an exceptionally significant college professor,
a poetic mentor
and a good friend who continues
to be an inspiration

and also to
all the living and deceased
Benedictine Monks of Conception Abbey,
who once were my teachers.

Author's Acknowledgment

Recently I read a book review in which the reviewer ended his comments by saying, ". . . this book needs an editor!" As I read that stinging closing statement, I gave thanks for my longtime editor, Thomas Skorupa. I am truly graced to have such a dedicated and creative editor who has also been a good friend for over twenty years. In the editorial process, he and I can engage in fiery creative disagreements that always conclude with a delightful harmony of minds and spirits. I also want to acknowledge those others who by their reading of the original manuscript have assisted him.

Having one's literary work edited is for an author akin to surgery without anesthsesia. An angry Thomas Jefferson knew the pain of such surgery. He referred to the eighty-six editorial deletions and changes made to his original text of the Declaration of Independence by the Continental Congress as "mutilations." While the operation of editing often feels to the author like mutilations, it is usually necessary if a manuscript is to become a book worth printing.

So I want to acknowledge with gratitude all those who have been involved in the editing of this book, including the readers who both evaluated and gave editorial suggestions on the first manuscript: Thomas Melchior, Carol Meyer, Ralph Sturm, along with Fred and Carol Eyerman. While they are friends, I appreciated their honest criticism and suggestions.

I wish as well to thank my publisher, Thomas Turkle, for his willingness to release this and the other books I have written, since at times they whirl wildly on the outer rim of risk.

Finally, I wish with gratitude to acknowledge you, the reader; you are so significant since this book was written for you! To you and all those named above — my gratitude.

Table of Contents

Foreword

Poetic Prayer

This forward is offered because the majority of contemporary prayers for both private and public worship are prose and not poetic in style. Prose prayer tends to be heard more by the mind than the soul, addressing the intellect rather than the heart. Poetry is that beautiful form of speech that sings to heart, mind and soul, and so helps the whole person to pray.

Before the psalmists of the First, or Old, Testament ever took up a pen to write, the Israelites, like other ancient peoples, had expressed their prayers to God in a poetic, lyrical form. The Israelites adopted from their neighbors in the Near East a style of poetry whose form and meter could express the language of their communal soul.

Poetry was an important part of every area of Hebrew life. Even their workaday prose was sometimes elevated by touches of poetic images and verse. Songs of work, drinking, harvest and love were woven into the fabric of daily life. Solemn occasions like engagements, weddings, the naming of a child, funerals and the harvest feasts absolutely required the use of lyrical expression. Blessings and curses were always in poetic form, and their folk wisdom was expressed in a style similar to our saying, "An apple a day keeps the doctor away." The Psalms attributed to King David were thus, not rare lyrical exceptions, but flowed out of the people's poetic expression in the midst of daily life.

It is in harmony with these ageless prayer traditions of the human family that the following psalm-song-prayers are offered to you. The reflections that follow each psalm are intended as commentaries and background. (You might want to reread the psalms after reading the reflections.) It is the psalms' lyrical and musical expression that will most fluently speak to your mind, heart and soul, helping to involve all your person in your prayer.

Chapter 1

Emigration for Those Who Never Leave Home

 Emigration involves moving from the known to the unknown, even if we never go to a foreign land. While some emigrate by choice, going in search of a better life, others are sent away, condemned by circumstances. Emigration from the familiar to the unfamiliar can also be set in motion by sickness, divorce, the loss of a job or by happy events like beginning a new work or being married. Emigration occurs whenever we move from one stage of life to another, from childhood to teenage years, young adulthood to mid life, then to old age and the final emigration — death.

This book of psalm prayers is for all of life's emigrants and is designed for those who will someday emigrate from planet Earth to a new life in space. Such a major migration requires more than space technology. Minds and hearts must be enlarged, purified and unified so as to live in harmony in space colonies composed of peoples of different races and religions — or of no religion.

Over 350 million years ago creatures in the oceans of our planet began to emigrate out of those primal ocean-wombs onto a hostile land. These ancient fish and early life forms, in search of a better place to live, were forced to take from their first home what they required to survive for brief periods out of the water. Over time these fish who flopped onto the planet's alien shores adapted to their new waterless environment until they no longer needed to return to their ocean home for food and oxygen.

Life is once again emigrating from a safe and known environment to a hostile one. Humans are taking brief trips off Earth out into the sea of space. History is repeating itself in preparation for the day when humans will be able to live in space stations and colonies beyond Earth.

Astronauts and cosmonauts are heroic emigrants and explorers who travel in high-technology spacecraft to explore the new world of space. Yet, centuries from now these spacecraft and the space stations that follow them will appear as crude as the ox-drawn covered wagons of pioneers or the sailing ships of Spanish explorers.

From the most primitive time to the present, humanity's history has been one of continuous emigration and exploration. America is a nation that has been largely formed by emigrants who departed from various homelands with diverse cultures. They came to a new land where, by necessity, they had to adapt and create a new way of life. Many of them did not emigrate freely but were deported as condemned prisoners.

The majority of those early emigrants knew they would never see their homeland again. With faith in themselves and in their God, with burning hope for a better life, they said farewell to all they loved, and departed, in the words of my Irish emigrant great-grandfather, "to fly with grandeur."

The State of Earth's Gravity

All life on Earth has evolved to live at 1-G, or *gravity one*. If you place this prayer book on a table, it will be held in place by the force of 1-G and will remain there until you move it. Drop this book, and 1-G will cause it to immediately fall to the floor.

On the other hand, *zero gravity* is the standard experience of space explorers. If this book were taken aboard a spacecraft and placed on a table, it would float in the air or travel wherever the space currents might take it.

It is taken for granted that 1-G is the normal state of life on earth. 1-G allows us to go about daily life with predictability: We drink our coffee by tipping our cup and allowing the coffee to flow into our mouths. We never doubt that the coffee will stay inside the cup until we're ready to drink it. We never suspect that the water from our showerhead might fall up.

Those who even briefly emigrate to space and its field of gravity must learn how to live in an alien environment. They are required to relearn even the simple act of moving from one place to another and need to perform the most ordinary of life's chores in new ways. As of this book's publication date, the long-term effects of zero gravity are not fully understood, but we do know that it alters emotions, mind, spirit and body.

The State of R-G

Daily life creates other forms of gravity that are also taken for granted until sickness, divorce, the death of a life-companion or the loss of our lifework cuts us adrift from R-G, the *gravity* of *routine*. Like Earth's gravity, R-G also forms a magnetic field for life on this planet.

Falling in love is an expression that well captures the absence of R-G, the gravitational field of the ordinary. Having the earth pulled out from under us by being in love is one of the more delightful forms of gravity loss and of emigration. In varying degrees, R-G is also lost when starting a new job, becoming engaged or crossing over one of life's borders at such ages as twenty-one, forty or sixty-five. Each of these experiences can cause a temporary loss of grounding, making us emigrants into zero gravity. They can also be adventures, explorations of new lands or — as in the case of deported criminals — a form of painful exile.

The State of R+G

The letters R and G can also signify a special kind of gravity which is created by our religion. R+G is represented by such religious symbols as the cross of Christ, the crescent moon of Islam, the wheel of Buddha and the Star of David. Ancient rituals, memorized prayers and scriptures known by heart ground us in our tradition. As valuable as our traditions are, the grounding they provide can make us feel comfortable by making God predictable. Yet God's nature defies predictability or being held captive by the gravity of churches, synagogues, mosques, temples, meeting houses or by theological labels and dogmas.

Again and again in human history, God has taken away the religious gravity of some women and men and caused them to enter a form of O-G, *out-of-groundedness*. Like someone falling in love, these persons have fallen out of their well-grounded religious traditions and radically into God, a state of spiritual zero gravity where up is sometimes down and down is sometimes up.

When gravity advances from 1-G to a billion-Gs, strange things begin to happen: A beam of light bends like hot licorice, and if the pull of gravity is increased to even greater strength the beam of light boomerangs back to where it began. When gravity is sufficiently strong, nothing can escape it. Even light disappears in what we call a black hole.

Prophets, visionaries, saviors, scientists and mystics have all experienced being swept away from their religious grounding. They've experienced something akin to being taken into a black hole — being consumed, as it were, by God. In varying degrees they've become accustomed to and have enjoyed their new weightlessness. So freed, they've gone about joyously proclaiming their new state of having fallen into God; others, desirous of also experiencing such freedom, have followed them.

With the passage of two or three generations, however,

disciples of the free-floating masters have usually longed for the gravity of predictable divine encounters. Therefore, numerous R+G traditions, with their appropriate religious symbols, have been established.

Yet God is freedom from all gravity and all predictability. God is eager to visit and invite brave spiritual explorers to become gravityless emigrants of the Imageless and Unimaginable God. Those who prefer that the ground always remain beneath their feet and that God remain predictable would be prudent to refrain from answering the door should God happen to knock.

R-G, *routine gravity*, and R+G, *religious gravity*, are magnetic forces we take for granted as much as we do 1-G. As all space pilgrims know, it can take some time to acclimate to weightlessness. This book of psalm-prayers is intended to help you respond to the absence of various forms of gravity. Hopefully, it will even help you enjoy the state of spiritual zero gravity.

I. Psalms of Prayer

While every psalm is a prayer, it is important to bring an attitude of prayer to every psalm in this book. The more common any action, the more routine it usually becomes. The habit of prayer can be beneficial, as it strengthens our connection to God as the ground of our lives. Yet it can also be dangerous since habits often lead to absent-mindedness. The humble plea to want to pray may be the best way to initiate prayer, as well as being a prayer in itself.

While it is common to speak of praying *to* God, prayer is more an act of being ushered into the reality of God. Prayer is entering into the presence of the Divine Mystery, which for the prophet Isaiah in the temple was a terrifying experience of the Holy, Holy, Holy One. At first, the prophet excused himself from being God's messenger, saying he had unclean lips. However, Isaiah had his lips cleansed with a red-hot burning coal which a six-winged angel carried in a tong from the altar of incense.

Each of us who sends a message of prayer to God could echo Isaiah's excuse. Indeed, a sense of awe, wonder and unworthiness should usher in each act of prayer. Before you pray, consider the simple ritual of making the sign of the cross on your lips, saying:

O Pure and Holy One, purify my unclean lips
as I now enter into your holy, holy presence.

The following psalm prayers are intended to assist you in the sacred act of praying.

1

The Agnostic's Psalm

Before I begin to pray,
    I recall the words of St. Thomas:
"I will never believe
    without probing the nail prints . . ."
and say with the father of the possessed boy:
    "Lord, I believe, help my unbelief."
My doubts about prayer have eaten
    a large donut hole in my soul.
So like an agnostic I come to pray,
    more hoping than believing
in the power of praying to you, my God.

No harm done by my time of prayer,
    yet does any good come of it?
Preachers say that you are unchangeable
    and that prayer makes me change.
Yet Jesus went so far as to say
    that if we pray with faith
mountains would change places;
    that if we knock the door would be opened.

I knock, O God, at your prayer door,
    my agnostic heart yearning to believe
that you hear my poor prayer
    and are deaf to my shaky belief.
For I trust that you listen with a lover's ears
    to one who longs to believe
in the awesome power of prayer.

Reflection: *In John's Gospel, the Apostle Thomas suffers from a lack of belief yet learns to believe (John 21: 24-29). In Mark's Gospel, the father of the possessed boy is aware of his lack of faith yet longs to believe (Mark 9: 24). Jesus, the Christ, along with the great spiritual masters, often pointed to the necessity of faith-filled prayer. Paradoxically, we see that acknowledging our doubt can be an important part of the process of coming to such a full faith.*

All prayer should be vested in faith in God, clothed in a belief and conviction in the power of prayer. Yet, how threadbare is so much of our prayer. Only a loincloth of faith and conviction begins and ends most prayer gatherings. Daily prayers that are only said instead of lived to the fullest are easily buried in the avalanche of approaching events. Such prayers are crisscrossed by jaywalking, wandering thoughts or pop-up rememberings of forgotten duties.

On the other hand, 911 petitions — disaster prayers — come fully attired with tearful, heartful pleading urgency. Yet such urgency should always be part of our prayer. We should always be aware of our utter poverty before God and of God's infinite love and mercy, as well as God's promise to hear our prayers. Thus we should never let our prayers go to God naked of humility and trust.

Before we pray, we need to properly attire each prayer in the golden vestments of faith and crown each word with conviction in the awesome power of speaking directly to the almighty and all-loving God. By acknowledging the doubt present deep within, this psalm helps us vest our prayer in the zero-gravity ground of faith that carries the heart and the mind to God.

2

Psalm of the Whole Body Praying

❧❧❧

O God, as I come to pray, be a mirror
in which I can see my whole Body.

In your mystic mirror, show me my real and entire Body,
so I can pray one with all the living
and with all who are fully alive, your saints.

Sacred Source of All Life,
in the Holy Spirit's full-length mirror
show me my whole Mystical Body
so that each time I pray, I can pray:
One with Christ, the Alpha and Omega, and all who
are one with your Risen One.
One with the Lord Buddha and all who
are one with your Enlightened One.
One with Mohammed and all who
are one with your Holy Prophet.
One with Father Moses and all who
are one with your Great Exodus Guide.
One with those of all faiths;
one with those of no faith.

In your Eden mirror, let me see my unclothed Body,
so each time I pray, I can pray:
One with your creatures who wear fur,
who have feathers, scales and fins.
One with all creation, with trees and plants,
with rocks and soil, water and mist.
One with planets, stars and space.

Each time I pray, let me see in your mirror,
my whole and holy Body,

so I can pray one with you, my God,
    and with all of you;
so each time I pray, I pray not only *to* you,
    but *with*, and always *in* you, my God.

 Reflection: *Even when a prayer is privately prayed, it is part of a chorus of prayer for and with others. No one ever prays alone. Each prayer is part of a cosmic chorus of praise, contrition, thanksgiving and petition. There is but One Body, and so all prayer is communal.*

You may be physically alone when you lift up your heart to God in prayer. However, your body does not stop with your physical body. The body whose eyes are reading this page is composed of cells, tissue, flesh, bone and skin, which determine the boundaries of your separate being. Yet from a larger perspective, your physical body is only a cell in a greater body, so vast as to be without edges or boundaries. Before you enter into prayer, always be aware of the entire body that is in prayer.

3

A Psalm-Prayer of Love
⇒⟫ ⟪⇐

O God who is Love,
    I begin my prayers as I pray for
  (name of spouse or child or beloved) ,
    whom I love with all my heart and soul,
and whose love for me is your greatest gift to me
    and your infallible presence between us.
Bless, help, guide and protect my loved one.

And on this day
   bless these my dear friends,
    (name special friends) ,
   whom I love and who love me,
with whatever they need
   for happiness, holiness and abundant life.

 Reflection: *Those in need rise to the top of our prayer intentions. Daily we are called to pray for family and friends: the sick and suffering, the dying and dead, the pregnant and the would-be pregnant, those riding the roller coaster of a wobbly marriage and those whom divorce has injured in its collapse. We remember all those who are struggling with pain or problems. If our loved ones are not in some particular need, they can easily be absent from our prayer.*

To pray for anyone is to be wedded to that person in the endless instant of God. Consider using the above love prayer as the headprayer, the archpetition, the leader of your parade of prayers. A love prayer is a mystical aphrodisiac of the heart, a stimulator of romance, an intensifier of love. A love prayer is a suspension bridge linking lovers over the mirage-canyon of separation created by distance or daily distraction, a bridge that links the lovers to the Lover as well.

A love prayer is an intimate love letter that is sealed with the hot red wax of the Spirit and that is hand-heart delivered as it is being prayed.

4

A Psalm to Enliven Habit Prayers
⟫ ⟪

May I invest each word of my spoken prayers
    with a whole and sincere heart.
With a heart full of fire,
    may I strive to live out all that I pray,
finding a musician's delight
    in the rhythm and sounds of my prayer words,
savoring the flavor of an unquenchable love
    in my prayers to you, my Beloved.

O Divine Mystery, may I pray best in my closet,
    hidden from view except from you.
May I feel the Spirit's spur in my side
    speedily rousing me to *become* my prayer.
May I feel the Spirit's wind filling my soul
    with a holy windmill power.
May I pray not only for what I know I can do
    but also for what I would long to do in you.

May my habit of heartfelt prayer
    bring me ever closer to your blessed side.

The Abridged Habit Psalm

My Beloved, save me from the treadmill of prayer!

Reflection: *Habits are life's well-worn paths that allow us to run freely down them since they are so well known, while less frequently traveled ways must be carefully treaded. Habits can be good, and habits can be bad. Good habits are patterns that make it second nature to be Godlike, to be holy. Bad habits, conversely, are prisons that*

incarcerate us in chains of reactions and thoughts that cause us as well as others pain and harm.

Praying memorized prayers, often learned in childhood, can be a good habit. Such prayers spring effortlessly to our lips. Habit prayers are as useful as 911 emergency prayers, which can race to our assistance in seconds when our minds are crowded with fear, helplessness or conflict. Take care, however, for habitual prayers can easily become empty boxcars rattling quickly by as we pray.

Indeed, not all prayers are fruitful. Bad-habit prayers, like bad habits in general, can also imprison us. Worship can be dangerous if it reinforces aged forms of prejudice and the ancient division between praise and justice. Prayers and rituals that only make us feel good and comfortable can be dangerous. Truly good prayer flows out in compassion for the poor and afflicted and feeds an ever growing desire for the removal of our self-centeredness.

Such compassion is Godlike, for it is a communion of emotion — of passion — with those who suffer and rejoice. Compassion is holy communion with our God, who feels the pain of prisoners, the rejection of those who are aliens to proper society and the rat-gnawing hunger of the starving.

5

The Answered-Prayer Psalm
⊰⊱⫷⫸

O *God, come to my assistance.*
"Friend, did you say 'Come'?
I'm already here beside you, inside of you!"

O Lord, make haste to help me.
"'Make haste,' friend?

I've never ceased helping you!"

O God, come to my assistance!
  "Don't shout, friend!
I'm closer to you than your own skin.

"Don't ring your prayer bell
    so loudly, my friend.
Be still and know that I am God,
    a God who is always for you
and with you — forever."

Reflection: *Our prayer postures proclaim our theology about prayer and about God. Head back, eyes focused upward, arms spread wide with palms raised to the heavens: These are all classic prayer stances that address a God who lives upstairs. Words also speak of prayer positions and dispositions. The traditional preface prayer in the Liturgy of Hours, recited or sung by clergy, religious men and women, begins with, "O God, come to my assistance." The response is, "O Lord, make haste to help me." These verses speak volumes about the posture of the heart in prayer.*

The body stooped down on bended knees with head hung low into cupped hands, or eyes that close as the head is bowed at the call to prayer, or a profound earth-hugging prostration — all these postures speak louder than any of our words of prayer.

Yet, what if every cell in your body is the holy of holies, a sacred temple of God? What if every artery in your body is a sacred river of the divine presence? What kind of position do you take to pray if you are totally consumed and possessed by the One to whom you pray?

God is in and part of, as well as up and out and beyond. Prayer positions of all sorts are valuable as long as your heart never forgets where the God to whom you pray really resides.

6

A Honey-Making Psalm
⋙ ⋘

O You, the Ever-Patient One,
    to whom endless petitions are addressed,
do my prayers bore you
    the way most prayers bore me?

You are eternally gracious
    not to fall asleep
as dull prayers
    parade endlessly before you.

Since I find them so tedious,
    surely they must weary you.
Share your secret of how I can stay awake
    amidst their endless, deadening drone.

I dose off during dull bee-rated prayers,
    the holy buzzing of eunuch bees
who can't make the honey of love
    and only buzz with blessed noise.
O God, spare me from lifeless prayer
    and let my heart sing vibrantly to you
in prayers honeyed
    with ever fresh passion and longing.

Reflection: *Too long, too boring—how many prayers are lullabies instead of love songs? Too intellectual, too theologically correct — how many prayers are lectures rather than exotic love poems? If you fall asleep during dull worship, does not God catnap as well?*

Make your prayers firecrackers that snap, pop and crackle. Strive to make your prayers like Roman candles that explode in a seemingly endless series of brilliant splashes of colored fire.

Never tire of trying to make your prayers like skyrockets that take off with a bang and soar upward, full of expectation, to the roof of the heavens, there to erupt in gigantic bursts of the splendor of an exploding galaxy.

II. Daily Psalm-Prayers

Daily prayer forms an important part of each of the world's great religious traditions. Although each religion calls its members beyond merely "saying prayers" to an ongoing life of prayer, the ritual of daily prayer is essential for creating order and meaning in the chaos of life. In deeply religious societies, prayer and worship begin and end the day and mark other specified times to create a daily rhythm.

For those living in secular and nonreligious societies, this ordering of the day by prayer takes on an almost "survival" quality since there are few social supports that help turn the spiritual seeker's heart and mind to God.

The following prayers are offered as morning psalms to help orient our hectic lives toward God at the beginning of the day. You are encouraged to use these prayers like recipes in a cook book. Add to, or subtract from, them with the freedom of any good cook who is following a recipe.

7

The Psalm of Sunday

Holy, holy are you, O God,
    and holy is this first day of the week.
On this leisure day, I unite myself
    with all who rest from their weekday labors.
I also unite myself in prayer today
    with those who worship you, their God,
in all Earth's churches and places of prayer.

O creative and loving God, on the seventh day
    you rested after your labor of love, creation,
and on the most famous first day of the week, Easter,
    you began a new creation.
On this day of the resurrection
    may I share in the renewing and regenerating life
that comes from resting in you alone.

Hear, O God, this holy Sunday prayer,
    that today's leisure and prayer
may fill me, body, mind, heart and soul,
    with your creative and life-giving Spirit.
I thus pray that all this week's coming days
    will be holy and freshly full of you.

8

The Psalm of Monday
⇒»«⇐

O God of fresh sunrises and new beginnings,
    I greet you on this first day of the workweek
as the great wheel of routine creaks round again
    with its cycle of work, tasks and daily chores.
Yet, renewed by the leisure and prayer of Sunday,
    I greet this new day as full of promise and hope.
With your grace and guidance, O God,
    I embrace whatever may come my way this day.

This Monday may well be full of surprises,
    filled with disappointments as well as appointments.
O God, whose work is making life out of death,
    help me turn my disappointments inside out.
Fill me with the faith to find within each disappointment
    an appointment with you and with greater life.

Help me to see interruptions as opportunities,
as messages from you inserted into my day.

Guide me to transform my failures into successes,
to bring fruitfulness out of frustration,
blessing out of roadblocks.
O Holy One, who works around the clock doing good,
show me how to go about doing good this day.

9

The Psalm of Tuesday
→≫ ≪←

O my Beloved, who never grows stale or old,
with prayer I dedicate this day to you.
Humble Tuesday, third day-child of seven,
is easily seen as commonplace, often tasteless.
May I invest this taken-for-granted day
with your ever-new youthfulness, O God.
Grant me the gift to see in all my activities this day
the dance of ever changing atoms
within Earth's secret life.

God of forever freshness and ever-original ideas,
inspire me to live this Tuesday with bright newness.
Creative Spirit, empower me, I pray,
to redecorate my routines and daily patterns.
Accompany me in redeeming this Tuesday
with love, service, compassion and fun.

10

The Psalm of Wednesday
❧

O God, you who are the Alpha and the Omega,
    the Beginning and the End of all being,
be also the Middle of my week and my life.
May midweek Wednesday be a midwife day for me,
    helping me to give birth to something gloriously new.
Poor Wednesday, sandwiched in this busy week,
    may I find within it countless divine visits.
Holding hidden epiphanies, sudden insights, within its folds,
    may it be for me a holy Wow Wednesday.

O God of Hide and Seek, who loves surprises,
    give me a peek at the new hidden inside the old.
Since life is like a many-layered onion,
    may I peel back a new layer this day.
O God, Ever-Present Beginning and End,
    help me this day to let some things end and others begin,
and to my delight may I discover a fresh face of you.

11

The Psalm of Thursday
❧

O God, Ever-Patient One, ever without distress,
    help me on this Thursday not to hurry.
Tomorrow is Friday, the finish line of the workweek,
    and I've so little time and so much to do.
I'm thus tempted to hurry through my day
    and not be mindful in my work, of those I love — or you.

May this be a mentor Thursday,
    instructing me that each time I hurry
I do violence to time and life;
    may it teach me that time is but you, O God, and Life,
divided by seconds, hours, days and months.

Holy community of saints in time's fullness,
    inspire me not to abuse the time-life entrusted to me.
Holy Community of Threefold God,
    remind me to hurry only in a grave emergency.
Holy God, gift me with the patience of rocks,
    of slate that is slowly surf-splashed into sand.
Holy God, gift me also with a lightning bolt's speed
    whenever I see you in others who are in need.
Help me, O God, to live each moment as holy time,
    to live each moment in you.

12

The Psalm of Friday
→》《←

Thank you, O God, for this day called Friday,
    the capstone workday of this week.
Thank you, O God in the name of Allah,
    for this day of prayer holy to all of Islam.
Thank you, O God, for giving me the dignity of work
    to balance and enhance the delight of play.
Thank you, O God, for this welcome caboose day,
    ending a train of five days of toil;
may I live it in a holy and mindful way.

I begin this Friday with prayerful thanks
    for all the blessings I've received this week.
With thanksgiving, I count the many times

you came to my aid with your help.
With gratitude, I rejoice at the lessons
    contained in my problems and mistakes.
I bow with prayerful wonderment at your many visits
    in my painful defeats and joyful victories,
for your presence in times of trial and loneliness
    as well as in times of tender love and prayer.
May I end this workweek, O God, in gratitude
    and in the same spirit of openness and expectation
    with which I tried to begin it.

13

The Psalm of Saturday
-≫≪-

O my Beloved, you who live without a clock,
    without a calendar of past and future days,
O my Friend of the Perpetual Now,
    how quickly these last six days have passed away.
O Divine Lover, within your intimate embrace
    all time flies, leaving only faded memories.
As Friday faded to join the parade of this weeks' days,
    may my labors and the love they contained
        be blessed by you.

May Saturday Sabbath, holy alarm clock day,
    awaken me to how very brief is my fleeting life.
May the seventh day loudly ring its life-alarm
    to shock me from my slumbered sleepwalking.
May this holy end-day jangle me awake in joy
    to see within the commonplace events of this day
    the end and purpose of my life.
Beloved God, help me to live this Saturday
    with great delight and fullness of life.

III. Morning Song-Psalms

For peoples of all cultures and all times, morning has been a prime time of prayer. Perhaps this is because the miracle of sunrise and a new day awakens the wonder of God in those with sensitive hearts. Even birds break into ecstatic song at daybreak.

Early morning offers a quiet time for prayer, before the clanking wheels of the workday begin to turn noisily around. Each morning's sun-kissed hands hold out the challenge to approach the various activities of the day in a fresh, new way. Each new day invites us to take into our hands the tasks of that day in partnership with God.

Our morning prayer can be as brief as a sign of the cross. This sacred sign dedicates the day to God, investing it with the sign of God's victory. To this we add a soulful and heartful "Amen" as we accept all that the day holds as an opportunity for prayer and praise.

The following psalms are songs to welcome the dawn of a new day. In Walt Disney's *Snow White* the seven dwarfs depart for work in the morning singing, "Hi ho, hi ho, it's off to work we go." Few of us leave for our jobs singing, or, if we do, it goes something like this, "O no, O no, it's off to work I've gotta go."

Morning psalm-songs can consecrate water into wine; they help turn the dull into the delightful, the routine into ritual, boredom into the kingdom — a life lived one with God. The following prayer-psalms are only starters; do not hesitate to create your own song in imitation of the seven dwarfs.

14

A Worker's Joy Psalm

⋘⋙

My Friend, hear my prayer.
   I fear today's plate is too full;
   too long is my to-do list
with its down-to-the-wire work;
   so I need your help.

Dear Friend, as you are continually calling me
   to share in your life and work,
I now invite you
   to come and share with me
every work and event of this my day,
   the scheduled and expected things,
as well as all the unexpected.

Beloved Friend, help me to load my every task
   with a full-hearted love
and remind me of this prayer throughout the day
   so each labor may be a source of delight,
an occasion of playtime with you.

Reflection: *When asked about how one found holiness in the midst of daily life, the fourteenth century German mystic, Meister Eckhart, said, "Wisdom consists in doing the next thing you have to do, doing it with your whole heart, and finding delight in doing it."*

Blessed are those seekers of the holy who can enter each day with the intention of doing whatever must be done with a full heart and a desire to delight in doing it. Blessed are those who find play in their work, for in doing so they enjoy friendship with God.

Woe to those who separate their playtime from their worktime and their love time from their prayer time, for they shall be doomed to boredom.

15

The Break-In Psalm
➤➤➤ ⟨⟨⟨

Beloved God, who protects and defends me,
    as I prepare to leave home for work,
gift me with the creativity
    to deal with a break-in.

I pray, O God,
    that you protect my home from thieves
who would violate my home and me.

Prepare me for all kinds of break-ins
    that might come my way this day:
the unexpected and disturbing theft,
    the pilfering of my peace,
from my well-ordered day's agenda.

Help me search for the prize
    hidden within your sur-prize visits.
Grant me the vision to recognize the Visitor
    wearing masks of troubles, delays or interruptions
so I may playfully make my day
    into a holy treasure hunt.

Reflection: *So intimate is our living space that when thieves break into our home we experience a sense of physical violation, a rape of our privacy. Thieves take away more than material processions.* They also carry off treasures of the heart: our feelings of security, privacy and the hallowed sense of our personal possessions.

As thieves can break into your home, so also God can break into your well-planned day with an unexpected problem, breakdown or interruption. Instead of being angry when your agenda is broken into or time stolen from your clock, consider unwrapping the surprise disaster to seek the prize hidden in it.

A well-oiled, smoothly running day often leaves little space for God. Many of us aren't likely to encounter God in our "normal gravity" days. Still, God does not will the break-ins of our home or schedule. An ever cunning and clever God, however, hides in break-in sur-prizes for those with eyes to see.

Everything in your daily life, including your response to break-ins, can be an act of devotion and a spiritual exercise, since the practical life and the spiritual life are one.

16

Psalm of a Concealed Weapon

y Beloved, my Friend,
    I begin this new day in prayer,
asking you to protect me
    from any harm to body and soul.

I acknowledge, my God, that at times
    I've carried a concealed weapon

— sometimes even concealed to me —
a loaded gun of hair-trigger anger
that potentially is lethally dangerous.

Merciful God,
help me not to injure others, or hurt myself,
when I am caught off guard today
by those who might cross me.
Remind me often of the cross of Christ, my teacher,
that I might learn to cultivate a nonviolent heart.

Disarm me, I pray, O God, and help me confess
the hidden anger I carry concealed
so that others, and I, will be safe in you.

 Reflection: *The fifteenth century Moslem mystic, Kabir, wrote, "Go over and over your beads . . . but when deep inside you there is a loaded gun, how can you have God?"*

While some countries and states legally allow the carrying of a concealed weapon, Jesus and Buddha forbade the possession of anger, whether out in the open or concealed. Concealed anger is extremely dangerous — both to the owner as well as to those who may be suddenly exposed to it.

Disarm yourself now at the beginning of this day. Go about your work and the day's activities wearing an empty holster and God will ride sidesaddle with you. If you feel that you are carrying no concealed weapon of anger or any other vice, consider taking a few moments in prayer to carefully search yourself, especially the inside pockets of your heart.

IV. The Bell Psalms

Some of the Psalms of David indicate that they are to be sung, accompanied by a harp or some other instrument. Similarly, the following psalms can be accompanied with a small hand bell, one of the primal instruments of prayer.

Prayer and bells have been married for over two millenniums, a marriage, so it seems, made in heaven. For thousands of years monastery bells have been rung to announce times of prayer. Tibetan Buddhists use prayer bells, and bells once hung from the hem of the high priest's vestments in the temple in Jerusalem. Bells were used by Irish saints, like the famous Saint Patrick's Bell, which today is an official relic. Church bells once pealed three times a day to announce the Angelus prayer. People began, ended and paused in the middle of their work and prayed this prayer to Mary, the Mother of God.

In the contemporary Western world, bells in church towers are still rung to announce the hour of worship and prayer. Bells are joyously rung at weddings and other celebrations, and tolled slowly at times of death as signs of mourning.

These ecumenical instruments of prayer and worship have had secular uses as well. In the days of walled cities, bells were rung at sunset to proclaim the closing of the city gates. They signaled the 8 P.M. curfew, from the old French *couvrefeu*, meaning "to cover the fire," and so announced the time to go to bed. School bells historically have signaled the end of classes, and bells have been rung in times of alarm, fire, war, break-ins and other dangers, even at the approach of tax deadlines. Evil spirits and demons were once believed to flee at the sound of ringing bells. Likewise, cathedral bells were tolled to ward off storms and lightning.

The expression "passing bells" refers to an old practice of ringing bells when someone was dying. Bells were sounded at the passing of a person's soul to guard it from being snatched by evil spirits. The passing bell also called anyone who might hear it to pray for the dead person's soul and its safe passage to paradise.

The following section of psalms continues the rich and deeply rooted tradition of bells calling us to prayer at significant life moments. Consider obtaining a good bronze bell with a clear ringing tone to use with these bell psalms. If this is not possible, substitute any small hand bell — or a well-tuned imagination.

17

A Blessing Psalm for a Prayer Bell
⇒⟫⟪⟫⟫⟪⟪⟫

Come, Holy Spirit, and bless my prayer bell,
    hallow it as a holy bell
to disperse any evil and harm that may threaten me.

(The bell is lifted up in cupped hands.)

As hallowed bells
    once warded off storms and pestilence,
roused wills to extinguish fires
    and hearts to fervent prayer;
as passing bells once thwarted evil spirits
    and called mourners
to surround a dead person with light,
    may the ringing of this prayer bell
likewise awaken in me
    all the powers of the Holy Sanctifier.

May my bell, blessed by your Spirit, O God,
    awaken my fearful, doubting heart

to your perpetual protection in my life,
　　to the awareness that love is stronger than evil.

At the sound of my little hallowed bell,
　　may all evil and all harm depart from me
— powers of darkness and destructive storms,
　　demons of devilish doubt and fear —
as I place myself securely in your arms,
　　my Beloved and Almighty God.

(The prayer bell is rung at the conclusion of the psalm.)

 Reflection: *This psalm is a blessing prayer for a prayer bell. It can also be recited when the shadow of evil falls across your life and in times of great fear.*
Traditionally, prayers for protection in the midst of storms have been recited while lighting a blessed candle. This hallowed bell psalm can be used to support such a light blessing — and to bring together words of prayer and ritual actions.

As mentioned in the forward to this section, your bell can be used as a "passing bell" when death approaches someone you love. This psalm is also intended to accompany such times of passing.

18

The Preface Prayer Bell Psalm
◆≫≪◆

(The prayer bell is rung at the beginning of the psalm.)

waken, O sluggish and dull heart,
　　hypnotized by problems and concerns;

awaken to the sound of my prayer bell.

(ringing of the bell)

Rise from your slumber, O my soul,
    and dress yourself in fiery love,
so these my prayers might be prayed
    as brand new, as if never said before,
with the fresh joy of New Year bells.

Holy, holy, holy are you, God of Hosts,
    of blinding beauty and glory.

(ringing of the bell)

Heaven and Earth are filled with beauty,
    for your glory fills all that is.
Blessed am I to come in your name,
    bowing down before your infinite holiness
as I now adore you in this time of prayer.

(The prayer bell is rung at the conclusion of the psalm.)

 Reflection: *This is a preface prayer to your usual daily prayer. It can also be recited by itself as a brief morning prayer. If used in this way, you may wish to add the following prayer before ringing your bell or at the end of the psalm:*

I dedicate to you, O God, all I will do this day,
    so that all my works and deeds,
    all my thoughts and speech,
    all my bodily movements and actions,
    all my encounters and dealings with others,
will be my continuous prayer of praise to you.

19

Bell Psalm of Petitions

⇒》《⇐

(The prayer bell is rung at the beginning of the psalm.)

Attend, O my God,
    to the sound of my cry,
as I your servant call out to you,
    coming with holy confidence before you in prayer.
May the ringing of my prayer bell awaken as well
    all the heavens, all the angels and saints.
I call upon all of the holy ones
    to intercede with you, my God,
to grant my humble personal needs:

*(The prayer bell is briefly rung before and after you pray
   your intentions.)*

I lift up to you these persons and their needs:

*(Here mention by name the needs of family and friends.
Then end your list of petitions by ringing the prayer bell.)*

As the sound of my small bell resonates outward,
    fading into the distance,
may these prayers for those I love,
    travel to your divine heart.

O God, besides those I have remembered by name,
    bless all my family and all those I love.
Bless those who have asked me to pray for them,
    especially anyone I may have forgotten.
And bless those who have no one to pray for them
    and who are in need this day.

Blessed are you, Beloved God,
    who hears and answers our prayers to you.

Reflection: *Jesus instructed his disciples to knock at God's door — that it would be opened and their request granted. This bell psalm is meant to accompany that gesture of coming to God's door of prayer and petitioning for our personal needs and the needs of those we love.*

Frequently we are asked to remember someone in prayer, and such requests can easily be misplaced or forgotten. Special requests should be written down, if possible, at the time we are asked — and, if not, when we return home. This prayer reminds us how important it is to perform this sacred duty. Even with the requests we have overlooked, we still contribute to this essential work of the Spirit, praying for others.

Like church bells knelled in rejoicing or mourning, your prayer bell can be rung without words to express your feelings or prayerful petitions.

20

Psalm of the Liberty Bell Prayer
⋙⋘

(The prayer bell is rung at the beginning of the psalm.)

ear, O Lord, the sound of my liberty bell,
 along with my prayer that rings out
my personal declaration of independence,
  the liberty I seek from all that now enslaves me.

O God, rally all your forces
  as I now seek to be freed
from the crippling chains that enslave me,

the shackles that hold me tightly bound.

(ringing of the bell)

Ring out boldly, O bell of the brave,
    so I may heed your call to courage.
Give me a heart of strength and of faith
    to know that I don't stand alone.

With you, my Beloved, ever at my side,
    on my left and on my right,
going before me and following behind,
    I will escape my slavery.

 Reflection: *As you pray this psalm, think of a particular present slavery that holds you bound. I say "present," because on one level life is a continual emigration, an escape from one prison after another. All of us human beings, in more or less subtle ways, embrace successive forms of slavery.*

These forms of enslavement are countless: negative attitudes, fears, the need for social approval, low self-esteem, drugs, alcohol, work, TV and various forms of entertainment — not to mention institutional and corporate colonization of the individual. Blessed are those who spend their entire lives escaping from one prison, one enslavement, after another.

The true independence and the glorious freedom of the children of God, spoken of by Paul in Romans (8: 21), is a liberty found in being exclusively a prisoner of love.

21

The Gloria Bell Psalm

(The prayer bell is joyfully rung at the beginning of the psalm.)

Don't check your calendar, Beloved God;
    today's not Easter Sunday.
But my gloria bell rings out joyfully,
    "Glory to God in the highest,"
as I rejoice in this little Easter,
    this small triumph in my life.

My thanksgiving prayer is soaked
    in the sunrise of resurrection joy,
all dressed up in new Easter clothes,
    to celebrate your gift to me of this life-success.
As you raised Jesus out of his tomb,
    so you've raised my hopes and my heart this day.

These little victories in life, my Easter God,
    I dedicate to you in the Spirit of the Risen Christ.
I celebrate with you in great yet secret joy,
    as at a lover's private party.
So my gloria bell rings only for you
    and all of heaven's saints and angels to hear.

(The prayer bell is rung as the prayer concludes:)

Glory to God in the highest;
    may glory fill my heart on this joyful day.

Reflection: *The name of this bell psalm comes from the first word in the old Latin Easter hymn, "Gloria in Excelsis" — in English, "Glory to God in the highest." It is also called the Angelic Hymn*

since it was the song of the angels at the birth of Jesus in Bethlehem.

Troubles and problems — whether our own or those of others — are the usual focus of our prayers. Life, however, is balanced by our successes and victories. Life's achievements, the successful completion of projects, acknowledgments by others of what we have done, promotions — even minor successes and victories of life — need to be celebrated.

The major accomplishments of life are usually accompanied by some family or social acknowledgment. However, personal and daily achievements are easily overlooked. This psalm allows you to celebrate and to be proud of yourself — yet in the manner proposed by the Master Jesus: secretly, with a meek and humble heart.

22

The Creation Bell Psalm
❧➤➤〈〈〈❧

(The prayer bell is rung at the beginning of the psalm.)

May my bell of the holy ring out loudly,
    O Spirit of Creation,
to inspire me to use the gifts
    of creativity and imagination
that you, my Generous God,
    have planted in every person
and particularly those holy gifts
    you have seeded in me.

(The prayer bell is briefly rung again.)

May my bell of the holy ring out, O God,
    to banish the demons of self-doubt

that try to hold my creative gifts captive,
    chaining them in the prison of the dogma
that it is only fortunate others who are creative.

May I use my creative gifts
    to bring joy to those I love,
to serve those in need
    and to give you, O God, great glory.

 Reflection: In the Bible, the first information we learn about God is that God creates. In Genesis, God creates with great variety and great delight day after day. All children enter life as creative artists, with vivid imaginations. We all share in the creative gift of God. This essential creativity is more fully acknowledged in some less technological cultures, where everyone is expected to be an artist in some way, whether that expression be music, carving, the preparation of food, fabric-making or dance.

When creativity is abandoned for various reasons as children grow into teenagers, violence often rushes in to fill the vacuum. Some scholars maintain the amount of violence in a culture is in direct proportion to the absence of commonplace daily creativity. If we do not desire to participate in destruction, we need to recapture our creativity. To create not some great masterpiece but a delicious dinner, to redesign a living space, to help solve a problem at work or school, to make up a game with your kids — or any expression of creativity — is to redeem your childhood God-gift.

Other Ritual Uses of Your Prayer Bell

Because of the unconscious association of bells with prayer and worship, the sound of a prayer bell becomes an unspoken prayer. The ringing of your prayer bell can be a wordless yet holy way to begin and end a day. It can dedicate the beginning and completion of any work or activity — even making love — in which you desire to be in communion with God.

A dinner bell sings out, "Come to the table." To use your prayer bell for special — or even daily — meals announces that these times at the table are holy times. A brief pause of silence after the bell has been rung can provide space for each person, in his or her own way, to give thanks to God for the meal.

The various occasions and events that can be consecrated by the sound of your prayer bell are many. May the psalm prayers offered here be bell-calls for you to create your own.

Chapter 2
Psalms for Life's Journey

I. Pilgrimage Psalms

Among the psalms of David are several prayer-poem-songs for pilgrims traveling up to the temple in the holy city of Jerusalem. Pilgrimage is itself a prayer, a path-psalm on the road to a holy place.

Pilgrimage is a sacred act in all the world's great religions. The destination of these holy trips can be a holy city such as Jerusalem, Rome, Mecca or Benares. Holy mountains and sacred rivers are other magnetic destinations of the devout. The birth and death places of saviors and holy ones are also beloved places of pilgrimage.

Moslems have an obligation at least once in their life to make a pilgrimage to Mecca. In Jubilee years, some Catholic Christians continue the tradition of making a pilgrimage to Rome, Jerusalem or a holy shrine in their own country.

The holy ritual of making a pilgrimage does not necessarily require packing a suitcase and crossing an ocean, since Jesus announced that the holiest place — the reign of God — is *here*. To be a pilgrim requires only an act of belief in this truth proclaimed by Jesus. Thus, taking a walk around the block can become a pilgrimage — for those with eyes to see. Moreover, every pilgrimage, whether across town or across continents, exposes us to zero gravity and is an opportunity for us to trust in God as we leave the normal security of home.

Against the backdrop of the ageless tradition of pilgrimage, the following psalms are prayers for pilgrims who stay at home as well as those who travel afar.

23

A Pilgrim-Emigrant's Suitcase Psalm

God of departures, Holy One of the Exodus,
    Spirit Guardian of all roads and routes,
I am about to depart on a new adventure in life,
    and my bags are packed with both dread and delight.
The old is known, comfortable, safe and secure;
    the unknown is threatening and danger-filled.
O God of travelers and holy emigrants, help me:
    besides anticipation and appreciation,
what else should I pack?

Comfortable clothes of change — nothing starched —
    yes, I understand, and a change of shoes.
Comfortable hiking shoes for exploring with ease
    the strange, unknown, wild lands ahead.
Yes, and also my dancing shoes so that with delight,
    I can celebrate the wedding feasts I come upon.
Yes, a sturdy oak staff of love upon which to lean —
    the older the oak, the stronger the staff.

One dream-vision as my map, and the compass of prayer
    when fog hides the stars or eclipses the sun.

One medicine kit with patience tablets for delays,
   dried memories for snacks along the way
   and bandages for a sprained spirit after a fall.

God of departures and homecomings, may I go forth with
   the adventure-hungry heart of an explorer,
the faith of one homeward bound to you
   and with you, Beloved Companion,
as my navigator and guide.

Reflection: *As recently as the last century, riding in an automobile could be a hair-raising, hazardous adventure. Yet one of the greatest dangers for the modern pilgrim is the contemporary disease of* **commonitis**, *deadly to those who wish to experience God and life to the fullest. The heart of an explorer is embalmed by repetition, which can make driving or traveling today all too commonplace. The zero-gravity antidote to this disease is a healthy dose of an adventurer's heart and an openness to be guided and surprised by the Divine Companion.*

Yes, traveling today is easier than in previous ages, yet few pack wisely for the unexpected or the delightful. More than a change of clothing is necessary to pack for any journey — if it is to be an adventure with God as your companion. Leaving home, even simply to go to work or to the store, exposes you to zero gravity as it turns you into a temporary emigrant. On any trip, this prayer can prepare you for hassles and inconveniences as well as adventures and joys, reminding you to take your patience tablets lest some delay should deport you to Angerland.

24

Psalm of God's Guest
❖❖❖

Attend to me, O my God,
    look upon my needs and hear me,
and remember that I am your guest.

I am a pilgrim under your roof,
    as were my gypsy ancestors,
those wandering Exodus emigrants
    who were your specially chosen ones.
So, protect me I pray, O God,
    from all that threatens me this day.

O Holy Host, under whose roof I rest,
    wash my feet with your love,
anoint my body with scented oils
    and kiss me with your healing affection
to send me soaring like a love-crazed hawk.

Remember me, Divine Host, as your guest
    who sleeps in your tent,
who feasts at your bountiful table,
    delighted by your loving care.
As your pilgrim guest, my Lord and Host,
    one final favor do I humbly ask.

(Mention here a final prayer request.)

Reflection: *The cry of Psalm 38: 13, "Hear my prayers, O God, for I am your guest," should be prayed with the confidence of a desert bedouin. For desert dwellers, a host had the ancient obligation to care for every need of a guest. Sacred was the duty of hospitality, treating a guest as one would receive an angel from God. Sacred*

was the need to protect from harm any guest in your tent as if the guest were one of your family.

This psalm helps us remember to see ourselves as such a guest in God's tent. See the sky above you as God's tent — whether it is woven with gray storm clouds or with bright blue linen. Live in the confidence that your Host will be attentive to your every need — as long as you are a guest who knows who and where you are.

Live today as a guest among other guests in God's tent, careful not to be rude to the other guests of your Host. Be grateful to the Host for every gracious gift of life. Frequently praise the Host, whose delicious food is abundantly served to you and who treats you royally with constant care. Live as a pilgrim guest, and you will always be filled with gratitude.

25

Psalm of a Pilgrim Leaving Home
⋙⋘

Beloved God, how graced and gifted I am
    to be able to make a pilgrimage.
I rejoice and give you thanks
    for this gift of traveling to a holy shrine,
drenched in blessing because of the countless prayers
    and the fertile faith of earnest pilgrims.
May this anticipated pilgrimage awaken in me
    a sense of the sacredness of all places
but most of all of the space within me.

Bless all my preparations for departure;
    grant to me a true pilgrim's heart,
which prays in the midst of packing

and clothes itself with the blessed cross
worn for centuries by holy travelers who were intent
    only on the sacred center of a shrine.
Bless my eyes with desire to see the Holy,
    not pious wonders or make-believe.
Bless my ears to be eager to hear the Holy,
    not unctuous noise or rattled prayer,
so I can come home renewed in my faith,
    and deepened in my love for you.

My Beloved, as I prepare to depart, I pray
    that you would remind me during my pilgrimage
to take home a piece of the holiness of the shrine
    and to leave a portion of my own devotion
to enrich those pilgrims who will come after me.

 Reflection: *All shrines are holy pools where pilgrims drink deeply and so are able to return home refreshed in their faith. Shrines are also pools replenished from the canteens of the pilgrims who visit them. By their prayerful presence, pilgrims pour back into the holy place the power of their faith-filled devotion.*

As a sponge soaks up water, so holy shrines absorb the love and devotional faith of their pilgrims, making the sacred site even holier than it was before their arrival. Only God knows if more grace is left or taken away by a true pilgrim. A true pilgrim is not like a spoon that doesn't know the taste of the soup, but rather is like a sponge that absorbs the essence of the shrine.

Take care, however, for pilgrims can be mere pious tourists. Tourists usually come to some site only to view it, and sometimes even leave trash and graffiti behind. Since we are unconsciously trained from childhood on how to be tourists, most Western pilgrims today rarely rise above holy tourism. So, if you are going on a pilgrimage, try to learn how to be a true pilgrim. Perhaps the psalms in this section can assist you in learning the fine art of pilgrimage.

26

Psalm of a Pedestrian Pilgrim
-≫≪-

Holy Guide of all pilgrims, bless me,
   for I am about to depart on a pilgrimage
to the holy shrines in my own backyard
   and those along the path of my neighborhood.
Bless my two feet — though shoed like horses,
   shod with heavy leather soles —
that they might feel the tingle of the Holy Land
   in every step beneath them.

Train my too-fast feet to walk with a measured pace,
   to make each step a prayer
— slowly up and gently down —
   touching holy ground reverently,
in awe of the sacred, soft grass,
   even the holy, hard concrete and pebbled lane,
for holy, holy, holy is all the earth,
   saturated in your glory,
the holy shrine of shrines.

"Don't hurry," archangels cry out,
   "for a pilgrim's progress should be slow and stately
like a bride processing down the aisle
   as you seek your heart's Beloved Groom
on every street corner, at every turn,
   desiring to make each moment
the wedding day of heaven and earth."

Reflection: *Able to evoke spontaneous applause
and shouts of joy — so miraculous and wondrous
were our first steps. Then after mastering the art of
unassisted upright walking — to the shame of*

gravity — we moved on to skipping, running, dancing and even leaping. Yet before long, ho-hum followed ecstasy, and our feet forgot a toddler's joy. Walking merely became a way to go from point A to point B, and often as quickly as possible.

Solemn bridal entrances and other processions require the discipline of slow, conscious walking. Hurry is unbecoming to a bride and "unblessing" to a pilgrim. It's an unblessing to hurriedly walk roughshod over the blessed earth, for we are thus cheated out of the gift that transforms simple walking into a pilgrimage.

Brief but frequent neighborhood pilgrimages can hold as many graces as treks taken to far-off holy cities and shrines. All that is required for a neighborhood pilgrimage is to walk with full consciousness of what you are doing as you go around the block or from your car to the store. Consider going to church as a pilgrim. Climb the steps to your church with reverence and enter it as a shrine. Approach Holy Communion with the prayerful, slow, stately pace of a bride whose heart is throbbing with love, and you will be thrice-blessed at Communion time.

27

Psalm of a Home-Bound Pilgrim
➤➤《《

Hear me, O God, our Home and our Destination,
   the Beginning and End of every pilgrimage,
I am weighed down by duties, and light on cash;
   I can't afford to travel to Jerusalem or Rome,
or pilgrimage to some far-off shrine,
   so open the eyes of this poor pilgrim,
who is sadly forced to stay at home.

Your Messenger-Son Jesus said that here,

right here, is full of you.
Yet here, the common here of my home,
    seems bland and "blessedless."
So grant me the miracle of Jesus' eyes
    to see my here as awesomely abounding,
jammed-full, O God, with the grace and wonder of you.

Every room is the holy of holies.
Every drop of water, holy water.
Every window, cathedral glass.
Every door, the holy door.
Every rug, a prayer carpet.
    All is sacred in this shrine of my holy here.

Reflection: *We believe Jesus when he proclaimed that God's reign had arrived, but we find it difficult to live our belief. One of the daily practices of every disciple of the teacher from Galilee should be to try to see with the eyes of Jesus.*

When the vision of the reign of God in their midst had faded, Jesus' disciples began to make pilgrimages to the site of his death and resurrection in Jerusalem, or to the sea of Galilee. Yet when we have true pilgrim eyes, we can recognize the holy in every corner of our lives. "Let those with eyes see," Jesus said two millenniums ago (see Luke 8: 9-10). So what do your eyes see?

28

Psalm of the Miraculous Holy Waters
➺➤ ⫷⫸

O Jerusalem's sacred pool at Bethesda,
    whose hallowed waters healed the sick,

O Lourdes' miraculous spring
   whose waters wondrously cure cripples,
O Ganges, holy river of Hindu India,
   whose primal waters wash away sins,
what can you offer this poor pilgrim,
   homestuck and hungry for healing?

O Creator of healing waters,
   bathe me in the wisdom that all water is holy,
consecrated in the very beginning
   by your Holy Wind-Spirit,
poured into the holy water of oceans and rivers,
   making every bathtub a Bethesda,
every creek, river or raindrop a Ganges,
   every glass of tap water a Lourdes.

 Reflection: *Historically, among the many reasons for making a pilgrimage has been to seek healing for an affliction or suffering — and the waters of various religious shrines are renowned for their powers to heal. Yet all water is wet with the wonder of the Holy. All water is healing in its mysterious power to make not only plant life but all life to grow. Water heals the thirsty, soothes the body from the pain of labor and washes away the soil and grime of the day.*

We might wonder, then, what makes holy water holy. While holy water requires a blessing, is the blessing for the water or for those who use it? Perhaps we could think of the blessing of water as a cold shower to sober up those drunk on the dullness of daily water.

Jesus revealed the mysterious holiness hidden in common water in his parable of the final judgment. The Judge separates the goats and sheep, saying, "I was thirsty, and you gave me a drink of water" (Matthew 25: 35). When we unknowingly give water to anyone in need, we enter into paradise, freed of all our sins, healed of our crippling behaviors and cleansed of the sores from the leprosy of our mistakes.

29

The Cautionary Pilgrim Psalm
⋙⋘

The roads to the ancient shrines of the Holy Land
   are full of many dangers, so beware.
The road to the Spanish shrine of Santiago
   is renowned for its thieves and robbers, so beware.
The road to England's shrine of Canterbury
   has taverns crowded with pickpockets.
The roads to all shrines are dangerous, so beware.

The holy roads to Canterbury, Jerusalem and Rome
   are crowded with holy counterfeits and crooks,
with prostitutes, pickpockets and purse-snatchers, so beware.
   Beware, pilgrims who travel the roads
to Mecca, Mount Sinai, the Ganges and Mount Fuji,
   for they have clever holy pretenders,
pious prostitutes and pickpockets of the soul,
   so beware, and prepare, all you pilgrims.

The religious road to the high holy shrine of the Divine Home
   is even more dangerous; so, pilgrim, beware.
Beware of holy prostitutes eager to lip-service your soul,
   seeking your money or your obedience.
Beware of ordained pickpockets who steal your peace
   with pious fingers poking at you with guilt,
Beware of holy fakes offering a cheap, cardboard spirituality.

Yes, pilgrim, regardless of which road you take, beware;
   yet take heart and do not fear.
Let the Holy Guide show you the natural road home,
   to find wonder in ordinary earthy things
and to genuflect before the everyday shrines
   as you give your whole heart to your Beloved.

Reflection: *Life is the great pilgrimage, in which our shrine-destination is God — not simply a shrine honoring God. Yet just as ancient pilgrimage roads were once infested with bandits and thieves, so too is the life pilgrimage. Pilgrims, those with hearts open to the gifts and the blessedness of life, are vulnerable to dangers from every direction. Yet there is protection present right in the process of the pilgrimage when we let God guide us on the pilgrim path.*

The world's famous sites of the miraculous are magnets that draw pilgrims. While the roads leading to them are magnetically charged, a wise and true pilgrim seeks such powerful fields of attraction that lead to God's presence right where every pilgrimage road begins: at home.

30

Psalm of the Pilgrimage to God's House
⇒⟩⟩⟨⟨⇐

With joy, O God, my feet are taking me up
    to your house, to my church,
with the same joy as once long ago
    prayerful pilgrims ascended Mount Zion,
climbing to your holy temple in Jerusalem.

Holy is this weekly pilgrimage,
    the journey my heart takes
to be nearer to you, my Heart of Hearts, my Beloved,
    whose love for me is boundless and true.

Dressing for church, may I be vested
    in true pilgrim's clothes,
making every departure detail

into a prayer of praise and love
as my heart fills with anticipation
at meeting you, Beloved God.

May today's going and returning
be a pair of holy pilgrimages,
journeys to and from your two holy houses,
the shrines of my church and my home,
both houses of prayer and the holy.

 Reflection: *The very act of going to a church, synagogue or mosque is a pilgrimage and a prayer. Prayer and worship do not wait until we go through the church doors; they begin the moment we prepare to go to worship.*

Prayer and worship cannot simply be left to special or inspirational moments, or our hearts will drift away. Across the centuries we hear God's cry related through the prophets, "Their hearts are far from me" — a cry which should cause the hairs on the back of our souls to stand on end. Moreover, contemporary life, which is almost exclusively secular and commercially seductive, rushes in upon our souls with wave upon wave of the unholy washing them further and further away from the heart of the Divine Mystery. In the face of such cultural currents, we need to consciously expand our times of attentiveness to God's presence in our lives; we need to cultivate a rhythm of prayerful living. To practice a pattern of prayer and worship is to swim against the tide, bringing our hearts and consciousness again to God.

The daily pilgrimage of prayer is essential. Without ever crossing the threshold of our homes, by our journey of prayer we carry our hearts back to God. By our weekly pilgrimage to our church or place of worship we do likewise. Both of these actions are pilgrimages from our busy, demanding daily lives into sacred space.

II. Psalms of Aging

Life is the great pilgrimage and a lifelong journey. Aging is the slowest and, for some, the most painful of emigrations. Those who are departing from the land of youth on their way to death often attempt to disguise themselves lest others know that they are emigrating. In our world, as in the ancient world, many have perpetually pursued the Fountain of Youth in this or that new drug, hair dye or wrinkle-preventing cream in an attempt to stay youthful as long as possible.

Once upon a time, the farewell pains of leaving youth behind were softened by the respect and honor paid to the elderly. Once upon a time, when human memory was the only reference library for historical knowledge, the eldest were highly valued as treasuries of family and social history, as living books of folk history.

Old age is another state of life that exposes us to zero gravity. As we cross the frontiers of aging, we retain fewer and fewer moorings that grounded us in our youth and gave meaning and purpose to our lives. In retirement our self-identity often diminishes, our health and physical abilities decline and our friends and support systems die away. The following psalm-prayers are for those pilgrims and emigrants crossing the various borders of aging — and for those nearing the end of this significant emigrant's road. All of them are intended to help us adjust to the zero gravity of aging and to help us move closer to the Ageless One.

31

The Birthday Psalm
⇥⤞⤝⇤

O Ageless One, as I celebrate my birthday
    and prepare to cross another frontier,
be my companion, a sacred stowaway in my heart,
    as I cross the border of one age to another.
I clutch my birth certificate passport
    to be stamped as I cross over the line.
One year, another frontier, they're no different,
    one from another, just numbers growing,
yet each frontier brings me closer to The Frontier,
    the last border I must cross to be with you.

This birthday crossing will not be difficult, I know;
    across this dateline all will be the same.
The feel, the smell and daily routine of my new age
    will not really change — all will be the same.
What I do fear is what I'll find further on,
    for across the border blows an ill wind,
brown with old dust and dead leaves,
    reeking with smells of sickness and death.

Each frontier, like this birthday, brings me closer
    to the approaching Great Border Crossing.
Help me, O God of the Crossing,
    not to drag my feet across this boundary line.
Help me not to lie, pretending I've not yet crossed it,
    disguising myself as someone younger than I.
Help me to dance across this dateline,
    zigzagging, wildly drunk with a lover's knowledge
that now I am closer to being home with you, my God.

Reflection: *Long ago, common people never cele-brated birthdays. Commoners were considered to be of no account, and so birthdays were the exclusive property of pharaohs and kings. Some people long to return to the old days when only regal persons kept track of the number of their years — but not because they want to go back to that zero gravity kingdom of no prestige.*

Although few of us desire to count our years as we get older, each birthday is an occasion to pack up your emigrant's bag and cross a frontier. Surrounded by cake and ice cream, flickering candle lights and a lapful of gifts, you can make the crossing a celebration in preparation for the joyous birthday into the fullness of life — your deathday.

A toast to a happy crossing of the Great Border, which this birthday anticipates, would be appropriate before blowing out the candles.

32

The Older the Tree Psalm
⊷≫≪⊷

Those who are planted in God soil,
    who live lives that are holy and true,
shall flourish and bear fruit,
    well into their dim-eyed senior years.
Those who are just to others
    shall flourish like the most abundant
of palm, fig, apple, pear or orange trees.

Garden-and-Orchard God,
    remind me of the ageless truth

that those who are deeply rooted in you
   shall bear fruit in every season.
Even in their old age
   their sap will be life-giving.

O sink deep, my aging, twisted roots,
   into the dark, rich soil of God.
So nourished,
   may my elder limbs sag earthward,
heavy with sweet, full-bodied fruit
   for all the world to enjoy.

 Reflection: *David's Psalm 91 (verse 140) sings of hope for those who may feel their fruit-bearing years are over. Yet our elder years are more truly harvest time than our early or middle years. Elder years are not for polishing trophies but for dropping into the soil fertile seeds that will sprout exotic flowers full of promise of fruit to come.*

In the closing years of your life, whether you live in your own home or a retirement home, may it be named **The Orchard of Paradise***. Truly, the older the tree, the more the fruit.*

33

Disbelief in Aging Psalm

 God, I confess —
      I am an atheist
   when it comes to aging;
      I simply don't believe in it.

I am a heretic
   of the dogma of dying,
the lessening of life.

Each year of life,
   I try to realign my orbit,
my circling around the sun —
   drawing myself each year
magnetically closer
   to you, the Fire,
the Light of Lights.

Ah, yes, it's true:
   the older the wick,
the higher the flame,
   till all is flame.
No more wick,
   no more wax,
till all, all is flame.

 Reflection: _Virginia Wolf said, "I don't believe in aging. I believe in forever altering one's aspect to the sun." Today, use the sun as your polestar to guide you through the valley of wrinkles and liver spots, falling hair and failing sight. Fear no evil in the dark valley of aging, for goodness and joy shall follow like a shadow all those who are on their way to be consumed by the Fire._

Where does the flame go when the candle is blown out? Where does life go when it's extinguished? Energy cannot be destroyed, only transformed. So become a pyromaniac as you journey through life, setting fire to as many things and persons as you can. Daily, illuminate every dark and dreary place. Daily, light fuses on youthful skyrockets and rekindle the dying embers of elders.

Each time you look at the sun, smile and shine brighter.

34

Psalm to God, the Joy of All My Life
⋙⋘

I will go up to the altar of God
　　to sing songs of gratitude,
for God gives joy in youth,
　　joy in middle age
and the greatest joy in old age.

I go joyfully up to God's holy altar,
　　not in the chains of obligation,
bowing, foot-dragging dreary, to do some duty,
　　but to dance drunk in gratitude
before the Source, the Fountain of Joy.

Thank you, O God, for theftproof joy
　　and ageless idealism.
Thank you for the joy of work
　　well and honestly done,
for the easy yoke of obligations
　　that are embraced out of love.
Thank you, too, for the joy of wisdom,
　　gleaned from a glossary
of many mistakes and errors.

I will go up to the altar of God
　　who gives joy in youth,
in middle years and in old age;
　　I will go to God, the joy of my death.

Reflection: *David's Psalm 42, expressing youthful praise, was once recited by priests as they ascended the three steps leading up to the altar. Regardless of how arthritic the priests may have been, those words*

promised an evergreen youthful joy.

As the number of age-boundaries crossed begin to mount, a homesickness for a previous age can easily grow like a cancer, especially in a society that adores youthful beauty. Instead of joy, advancing age then ushers in gloom, cynicism and bitterness.

As an emigrant of aging, daily finger the gratitude prayer-beads of joy and delight in life. Look backwards only to find more beads to add to your rosary of gratitude. Each year as you climb another birthday step of God's altar of life, do so in joyful vigor.

III. Temporary-Emigrant Psalms

The title of emigrant is usually applied to one who makes a major life-transition, as did the emigrants who came to America from Continental Europe and Ireland a century ago. Emigrants can be adventurers who go to a new land in search of a better life, or they can be refugees fleeing oppression, poverty and pain.

Yet in our lifetime each of us frequently experiences being an emigrant as we move from one stage of life to another. In fact, any new situation can make us feel like a stranger in a strange land. We also become temporary emigrants in the midst of experiences like sickness, which momentarily remove us from the routine of life.

There are other times when we are emigrants against our will. Deportation is a form of transition in which we are unwillingly removed not only from our homeland but from the daily routine of life. The loss of a job and needing to begin new work can make us deportees, leaving us feeling alienated and alone. Making a mistake rips away the gravity of confidence and can be as unsettling as being thrown into zero gravity. As prisoners once became forced emigrants, so too clocks, schedules and our special fears — like public speaking — can turn us into deportees.

The prayer-psalms of this chapter are for those who find themselves to be temporary emigrants. Hopefully these psalms will help those who are making transitions in life to adjust to their special forms of zero gravity.

35

Psalm for a New Work
➤➤➤ ⋘⋘

O God of Newness and New Beginnings,
    hear this emigrant prayer of your beloved one.
New York, the Big Apple, is a great and awesome place
    with its skyscrapers, stores and bright lights of Broadway.
New Work, which I am beginning, is not such a great place,
    but is more like a sour, green apple.
O God, who is ever working on something new,
    help me, a beginner, to find joy in my new work.
For sometimes bitter is the taste of this task
    of undertaking a new and unknown work.

Now stripped of my old comfortable lifework,
    I feel exposed to red-faced mistakes.
A beginner once again, I fear the shadow of shame,
    for in any new task, making mistakes is part of the terrain.
O God who is never ashamed,
    who finds delight in nakedness, who has nothing to hide,
make me a youthful adventurer, who with joy and trust
    find myself a beginner, again.

Reflection: *As people who have journeyed from foreign countries find the language and slang, the customs and food of the new country different and difficult, so do those who migrate to a new job. Regardless of how often we may have taken up a new position, we begin as an alien who doesn't know the ropes.*

In the days of old sailing ships, seasoned sailors knew by heart the ropes that controlled the sails of those ships. Those going to sea for the first time were novices, new to the knots and ropes. They found their "new world" to be a land of embarrassment and a steep learning curve.

The major work of anyone beginning a new task or job lies in the area of making mistakes. We should strive to make errors as gracefully as possible. No one can make us feel embarrassed; it is a self-deporting experience. We exile ourselves to that foreign state. May this psalm and the one to follow help your graceful gravitation to a new work.

36

A Stranger in a Strange Land Psalm
→≫ ≪←

O my God, help me,
   for I feel lost in this strange place
and yearn to feel at home again.
Help me, O you who are truly at home in every place,
   to be at home in this unfamiliar space.

Stolen is my compass of comfort,
   my confident ground of the familiar and known.
Without that compass, my heart fills with fear,
   jettisoning my peace of mind and heart
and casting me adrift in a sea of strangeness.

O God whose home is here and everywhere,
   help this new place to be as comfortable
   as an old shoe.
May my awareness of your ever present love
   make a homeland
   of what now for me is strange land.

Reflection: *The compass of comfort points with confidence to the North Star of being in control. Entering any unknown space — whether a new country, a new office or a new experience —steals that compass as we step into the zero-gravity, high-anxiety space of feeling out of control.*

Yet to be conscious of the abiding presence of God in all places and at all times is to escape from this anxiety. It helps us realize that needing to be in control is living in an illusionary land. For are we ever really in control? To hand over your attempt to manage life, people and events is to discover the glorious freedom of never being a stranger.

37

The Psalm of Making Mistakes
⇒》《⇐

've lost my footing, am adrift in shame,
    for I've made a mistake once again.
Thunderous at my door are the repeated knocks
    of childhood recollections of blushing guilt,
memories of wrong answers, wrong actions.

Being right grounds me safely,
    three feet deep in the earth.
From there I can stand tall and proud,
    victorious in all the applause,
head held high, a gleam in my eye.

Being wrong, however, is being caught off base,
    striking out and being shamed-faced.
Help me, I pray, O God of mistakes,
    you who first outlawed all images of yourself,
then changed your mind and made Jesus your image.

O God who works to bring life out of death,
help me to work good out of my mistakes.

 Reflection: *Making a mistake can feel like being throw into zero gravity, cast adrift from normal gravity's foundation of being right. This loss of the gravity of assurance is so painful and shameful that* many try to deny their mistakes. Adrift in embarrassment, stung by shameful memories of previous mistakes, we might try to blame the error on some machine or other person. Yet by this pretending we make another mistake.

We might ask Jesus of Galilee, who had mistakenly chosen Judas as one of his inner circle of twelve, to help us embrace the awareness that all our choices may not be correct. That same Jesus of Galilee also mistakenly trusted that after his death his apostles would continue his all-inclusive, male-female, sinner-saint community of equality.

It is said that "all things work out for the good." This is true only if we labor with love to make good arise from failures and mistakes. Indeed, such transformation of mistakes is not magical, miraculous or instantaneous. Yet if we trust in God, our mistakes can be the rich fertilizer out of which beautiful, fruitful life grows.

38

Psalm-Prayer Before Public Speaking
❧❧❧

To assist in the transformation of the energy of anxiety into the fuel of success, the following prayer is offered. It can be recited as you symbolically wash your hands in water.

*C*leanse me, O God, of all fear of shame.
  Cleanse me, O God, of all desire for fame,
that I might be your word aflame.

Reflection: *Studies have revealed that, overall, people's number one fear is speaking in public. More than snakes, spiders, the fear of heights, the fear of flying or other dangers, speaking before others generates terrifying anxieties. All those who preach, teach or give presentations to any kind of group must confront this fear.*

The fear of shame and the desire for fame are twin enemies that work against anyone wishing to be a good speaker. Often the fear of shame is a childhood shadow that lingers into adulthood. The source of shame may have been an occasion in childhood when we became the object of laughter and ridicule because of some mistake. This fear may have been created without malice by those who simply found the event to be humorous. Sometimes, sadly, children or even parents maliciously induce shame by taunting a child who makes an error. Because its roots are so primal — going back to our first parents, Adam and Eve — shame is a difficult fear to shake.

The second public speaking temptation from which to be cleansed is the desire to be successful. While it is good to want to use our talents in the best way we can, the need for success is dangerous. It can be more lethal than the fear of being shamed. The addiction to being successful can cause a mispronounced word, a fumble or a long pause to be devastating.

Beyond public speaking, this prayer can be helpful before any activity in life. Each of us is a word of God made flesh, and in every action of love or deed of service and compassion we become the enfleshed words of God. Our primary desire should be to become a fiery instrument of God, so the divine will can flow through us freely without the blockage of excessive concern about making a mistake or being successful.

39

Psalm of the Slumbering Time Traveler
❧❦❧

Awaken me, O God, to this holy moment,
the hour of *now*,
so crowded with your presence,
this hour of now,
when the hands on my clock
pause in their relentless whirling
to point to you, my Beloved Friend.

Awaken this poor wanderer,
this watch-watching sleeper,
this walking emigrant of time,
so that no matter what I'm doing,
I will stop
wasting time.

Stopwatch me in my tracks, O God,
so I may escape the prison
of my poverty of having no time,
so I can fully awaken
to the treasures you have graciously jammed
— and to your timeless presence —
in this holy hour of *now*.

Reflection: *Those who are kidnapped are involuntary emigrants, and clocks kidnap us. Each hour, each minute, we are travelers with eyes glued to round-faced clocks, as the landscape of life flies by. Believing that the journey takes a lifetime, we routinely close our eyes to the beauty before us in the* **now** *hour.*

Three times in the Gospel of John, Jesus said, "The hour is coming, and it has already arrived." The reality of "already arrived" is the fullness of time that awaits us when time will end. The "already arrived" fills the present moment with the fullness of the divine presence.

Prayer time never ends or begins for the true pilgrim of the heart. Meditation is not a practice; it is the path. So, make your wristwatch into a stopwatch, a watch that stops time. If you can effect this transformation, even for only a few brief moments in your day, you will find that you are the winner of the race. You will already have crossed the finish line and will be standing in paradise.

40

The Pickpocket Psalm
➳⟫⟪⟸

Take care, O pilgrim,
    lest the hands of the clock
pickpocket your heart,
    stealing from you, unnoticed,
your greatest wealth.

While robbers love to lurk hidden
    in alleys and doorways,
pickpockets prefer crowds
    to ply their nimble-fingered trade —
and thieving clocks thrive on crowded schedules.

I, your Beloved Master, told you,
    "Now is the hour."
So I caution you to travel lightly —
    keep slim your agendas,

fill your schedules only half full.

Friend, be poor of commitments
    so that you and I
might make love in the empty corners
    of life's busy places
and so find our heartpockets ever full.

 Reflection: *Fat schedules with back-to-back commitments leave no time to accidentally meet up with the secret Beloved or to dillydally with the Divine. Be alert, for time travel is the most dangerous of all pilgrimages. As we travel across not miles but minutes, hours, days, weeks and months, we need to be especially cautious. Clocks are the natural enemies of love. For who makes love with a time clock? In the commercial world, however, worth is weighed in the scales of busyness. If you are not busy, then you are not productive or valuable.*

In the ancient time before deadlines, a work was to be completed when it was completed. Hurry-hurry, rush-rush, not tick-tock, is the sound of today's ever faster clicking clock. When trains became transcontinental, clocks were consecrated as holy objects, for trains had to run on time. Soon, so did their passengers and even those who lived alongside the tracks.

We live in a world of clocks, whose eyes watch out at us from television sets, coffee makers, radios and other appliances, whose hands reach down from church walls to carefully measure worship and prayer. Yet just as keeping time is essential to making music, keeping time in check is essential to making prayer and making love.

41

A Psalm of Deportation by Sickness

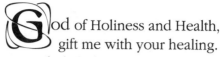

God of Holiness and Health,
    gift me with your healing.
I, your beloved one,
    have been exiled by my sickness,
to a place I did not care to visit.

Divine Healer, who graciously made me
    in your wholesome image,
gifting my body with the wonderful power
    to heal itself,
awaken, I pray, my physician within.

Heal all my inner conflicts
    that may block or clot
the flow of this interior healing
    so it may join with my medicine
in rapidly returning me to health.

Homesick for health, O God,
    I embrace this unwanted exile,
this state of discomfort, pain and suffering,
    asking that it remind me
to be ever grateful for good health.

Reflection: *Without leaving your native land, you temporarily may experience forced deportation to a place of sickness and suffering. These exiles may be brief or long lasting and are as bitter as vinegar to swallow. Most of us resent deportation by disease, protesting that we have too much work to do to be banished from the land of health.*

*This psalm can awaken us to our God-given inner power,
which can escalate our healing by modern medicine. When prayer
and medicine are administered with loving acceptance of the
temporary state of exile, healing, homecoming-to-health miracles,
can abound.*

42

Psalm of a Sick, Home-Bound Patient
➔>> <<➔

Germs — and not you, my God —
        are to blame
for my being deported by a virus
    to this ugly island
in the sea of sickness.

In the playing field of life,
    I've always tried to avoid catching
a cold, the flu, or any disease
    — always washing my hands and food —
but now, alas, a sickness has caught me.

An unseen little virus
    has hitchhiked a ride on me,
like a tramp on a freight train,
    and so now I am sick
with a secondhand disease.

My Beloved Healer,
    who only desires wholeness and what is good,
who is rightly praised by all things,
    let my aches and pains give you glory,
but make me well soon.

Reflection: *Among the secret herbs that heal, one of the most effective is also vastly underused: a large pinch of humor. Lightness and sickness, however, don't seem to go together, for who can find anything humorous in being sick with the flu or a head cold? Moreover, aren't psalms supposed to be somber, salted with seriousness rather than jest?*

Yet even a touch of humor can help turn things around. So, pray this lighthearted psalm, take two aspirins and get plenty of bed rest. To facilitate a rapid cure, if you, someone in your family or the family doctor know any good jokes, also take a healthy dose of them several times a day.

Chapter 3
Devotional Psalms

I. Love Psalms

 The First, or Old, Testament contains a beautiful book about love, the Song of Songs, attributed to that great lover, King Solomon. This love poem-song stands out among the other books detailing religious regulations for the daily life of God's chosen people, the prescribed rituals of the bloody temple sacrifice and accounts of an avenging God leading armies into genocidal wrath.

Aghast at the erotic nature of the poetry, some scholars have strived to justify its presence in the "Holy Book," saying that the lover in the Song of Songs represents God and that the bride represents Israel for Jewish readers and the Church for Christians. Those scholars and theologians who see no vice in human love, however, believe it was a bridal song of human lovers. Symbolic, literal or both, the Song of Songs appears as the only X-rated book in the Bible, and it was not to be read or heard by those of inappropriate age.

The Earth's hugging magnetic power of gravity is canceled out when one falls out of routine and tumbles into love. The state of being in love is remarkably like the state of being in outer space, where the absence of 1-G (Earth's gravitational field) requires learning how to adjust to a state of floating. Unfortunately — or fortunately for the practical minded, for those of us who focus on the serious business of life on Earth — acts of falling in love like space missions, are limited to short periods of time.

As today's space missions are the preparatory explorations for future life outside Earth's gravity, so also are the gravity-defying adventures of falling in love. Wise and blessed are those who are perpetual victims of love's loss of gravity, for they are more easily able to acclimate to zero gravity in all its forms.

As with the Song of Songs, the psalms in this section can be used as prayers to your Divine Beloved, particularly those directly addressed to that Lover. They also are psalm-prayers well-suited for lovers to express the mystery of their love for one another, which is a taste of the fullness of love in heaven.

The names for God used here — Beloved, Lover and Friend — are full of implications for the spiritual pilgrim and have a rich history in the world's mystical traditions.

43

The Bridegroom Psalm
❖❖❖

I blush a bit, O God, yet tingle with joy
   when Isaiah sings that you desire to come
with the passion of an eager bridegroom
   climbing into his virgin bride's bed.

Lover Lord, I am no virgin —
   in my soul, at least.
You are not the first one I've loved,
   for in many beds have I searched for love,

the kind of love to drive me mad.

As you love your bride Israel with great passion,
    come now and love me.
Love me into an incurable insanity,
    that care-less and unbounded happiness
of the simpleminded, saints and young lovers.

 Reflection: *Isaiah (62: 1-5) boldly speaks of God's passion: "As a young man marries a virgin, so God shall marry you; as with great joy a bridegroom takes his bride, so shall your God find joy in you."*

Seasoned lovers, made near-deaf by routine to the pounding heart-drums of love and numb to novelty in making love, can pray this psalm for the Spirit of the New to ever freshen up, heighten and deepen their romance.

Both earthy and spiritual romance need perpetual renewal and enhancing.

44

Song of a Modest Lover
⋑⋙ ⋘⋐

Y ou are a modest lover, O God,
    and I like that in you.
You never expose yourself for display
    in public or in private,
and I love that about you.

I love your subtlety, your never-nakedness,
    even when we are alone.
Even when we make love together,

you are carefully eclipsed,
and I love that about you.

I would explode in ecstasy
if I ever saw you truly naked.
The skin boundaries of my body,
as well as the margins of my soul and spirit,
would be wildly blown asunder
if ever you and I made naked love.

 Reflection: *God's nakedness is lethal to humans. Graciously, God makes love in the dark. Nor do we ever fully expose ourselves; none of us makes love completely naked. While bodies may be bare of clothing, we are draped in shadows of hidden secrets and deep fears.*

Atheists and agnostics demand that God perform a striptease, insisting that they will only believe if they see a naked God. Even to mystics, on this side of the grave our ever modest God wears a large fig leaf.

From this point of view, how might the kingdom of God appear when we reach the fullness of heaven? Paradise might just be a spiritual nudist colony!

45

Soft Wax Psalm
➤➤➤ ❮❮❮

Lover of Lovers, before you rise and leave,
squeeze me tightly in your farewell embrace,
for I am soft from the intense heat

of your passionately making love to me.
I'm as pliable as melted wax.

Embrace me tightly before we part;
    press deeply your warm fingers
upon my face and all over my body,
    leaving your holy fingerprints
all over me, like flaming tattoos,
    for everyone I meet to see.

Thus touched by you, Beloved One,
    everyone will know for sure
who is guilty of melting me
    into the madness of a teenage love.
Thus melted, my heart may more easily yield
    and conform to your holy heart.

 Reflection: *Mature people usually feel awkward and silly when they fall out of control and into love. Just as medicine lacks a cure for a sickness like cancer, there is no known remedy for being lovesick. The lovesick often act immaturely, having lost the gravity of being grave — that sad state of being too early in one's grave. They act silly when they should be serious, careless when they should be careful.*

Like drug use, the affliction of love can cause serious errors in judgment, disregard for thrift and behavior bordering on madness. It's no wonder that, like lovers, mystics and saints are judged by the Court of Reality to be "out of touch."

Every true encounter with God leaves the Beloved's fingerprints all over us. Yet, just as human fingerprints can easily be overlooked, so can those of the Beloved. Consider whether you prefer visible or invisible telltale signs of your encounters with God.

46

Psalm of an Incurable Patient
-»»««-

Beloved One, I am sick
and don't ever want to get well.
Friends and family will undoubtedly
urge me to take my medicine,
but I'll dump it down the toilet,
for I love being sick.

Sickness and pain being socially taboo,
they'll likely send me
to a doctor, two folk healers,
a wild Voodoo medicine man
and finally a Freudian shrink.

My affliction is a heart disease,
and its Latin name is *nostalgia.*
This primal malady called homesickness
is universal and deeply rooted.
The cures offered are all powerful drugs
including the strongest of all: religion!

Yet no medicine can take away this pain
short of coming home to you, O God.
So hear, O Beloved, my agonized groans,
being sick with you
and without hope of a cure,
yet also without even a desire
to see the sickness cease.

Reflection: *The entire population suffers from a God disease, which is not just contagious but prenatal. From ancient times the world has abounded in medical facilities — with names like*

temples, shrines and churches — set aside for treatment of the sickness known as nostalgia.

Research over millenniums has proven that small and harmless doses of the Source of the affliction provides temporary relief from the sickness. The sick who visit their local holy hospital for their weekly inoculations never call in sick at work and so never miss a day on the assembly line. Alcohol, money, shopping and drugs like television and work are used to mask the pain of nostalgia for those who do not make frequent visits to a holy hospital.

In recent centuries, some have tried to heal the sick by attempting to convince them that their sickness is an illusion, since no "home" exists for which to long. Those healers who deny the Source of the sickness have denounced the holy hospitals worldwide as the polluted places in which the virus has been spread, especially to the poor and lower classes.

This psalm is for everyone in love with this homesickness, for those who find its sweet suffering akin to the pain of passionate lovemaking. They refuse treatment and seek no cures. Instead, they are constantly searching for books, times, places and persons able to make them sicker, and so seek to intensify their pain.

47

Psalm of the Detective Eye
⇶⇶⇷⇷

Give me a mystical magnifying glass, O God;
 make great the eye of my heart
to see the trail of where you've been
 and all you've touched in your wake.

Magnify my bright heart-eye vision
 to see how I and all the Earth,

from the nearest to the furthest bounds,
    have been lovingly fondled by you, Beloved.
For your glowing fingerprints, O God,
    are upon everything in my house,
on each plant in the garden,
    on the morning and night sky,
and on my every deed and thought.

May I follow your endless trail with joy,
    with an unrelenting detective's passion,
until the trail ends
    in the fullness of you.

 Reflection: *Like Sherlock Holmes, spiritual seekers must train their eyes to search constantly for clues. Never glance, always focus. Never look, always see.*

Good disciples are detectives who relentlessly pursue the Invisible One who is guilty of stealing death. Each time they visit the scene of the crime — anywhere in creation — they are careful to touch nothing until they have examined it carefully with the great magnifying eye of the heart.

Blessed are those who do not just look, but who truly see, for they shall never lose the trail.

48

The Tavern Psalm
⇒⟩⟩⟨⟨⇐

I went to your tavern,
    intent on getting drunk.
Thirsty as an arid desert

was I for you,
as I hastened to the bar.

Inside the tavern
    I took a seat among
the gathered chatting crowd,
    yet few others — if any —
were there to get drunk.

I went to your tavern,
    intent on getting drunk
but was only served drafts
    of water-weak words
and nonalcoholic hymns.

Staying till it closed,
    I left your tavern dry,
still thirsting for you;
    my heart in my shoes,
I stumbled home sober.

Reflection: *The weekly wedding feast of worship is often the Wedding of Cana in reverse. The wildly intoxicating wine of the Bridegroom is transmuted back into plain water. Few complain about the un-miracle—many because they've come to expect nothing better. Others, members of the Prohibitionist Church, are relieved, since they find drunkenness to be the source of spontaneous dancing, loud laughter, and excessive expression of affection — especially in public.*

Blessed and fortunate are the thirsty drunks who know the road to the forest hideout of holy bootleggers. These women and men return home drunk on the Beloved. They have been known to abandon good jobs — and other things — being consumed by such drink.

Blessed boozers even know how to make home brew and are closet drunks, having been instructed by the Beloved to imbibe in the secret of their closets. They daily go to work dead drunk, cleverly disguising the divine odor on their breath. They only give hints of their addiction: slurred speech when words about God slip out or appearing to be tipsy in their trusting in the midst of troubles. Added to these telltale signs is the fact that these drunks smile too much.

Love being the most potent of all spirits, it's no wonder that the majority are in favor of Pious Prohibition.

49

Psalm for Dying of an Incurable Disease

Skilled at being my own doctor,
  I have diagnosed my disease,
that terminal sickness
  that consumes me.

No therapy or radiation
  holds out any hope.
No known surgery
  can remove it.

For I'm dying of anticipation,
  and so seek no cure.
I have no desire to delay, O God,
  making love with you forever.

Yet, wrenching is my disease,
  pulling me two directions:
wanting to be home
  with you;
wanting to be home
  with those who need me.

Suspended in this dilemma,
I lay open my heart
before you, my Beloved.

 Reflection: *Dying suspends us between two mighty magnetic fields of love and longing. Extremely powerful is this Earth's gravitational field, especially if you are young enough to still be needed by those whom you love and who do not want you to die. Equally powerful is the gravity of a billion-times-a-billion-G, the magnetic field between God drawing the beloved and the beloved aching to let go and go home to God.*

Life is the name of our existence on this earth. Yet life here is only a stage in Life. As the time of emigration to the next and final stage draws near, the beloved is torn between the duty to stay behind and the passion for ultimate consummation of his or her love of God.

Lovers do not dread death so much as they dread leaving those who need them. Yet in faith we know that we can do more good for those we love when we are in God then we ever could do on Earth. Those who die with pockets filled with that holy knowledge can say good-bye with confidence, then let go and be swept up into God.

50

Psalm of the Yearning Mountain Stream

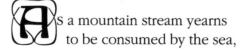

S a mountain stream yearns
to be consumed by the sea,

so do I eagerly pray and long
  to empty into you, my Beloved.

As a stream races over rocks,
  tumbling down the mountain,
so do I fall constantly toward you,
  Sea of Life and Endless Mercy.

As a leaping mountain stream
  stops not to gather gold nuggets
sprinkled in its streambed road,
  I seek only my treasure in the Sea of You.

As a stream gurgles in wet delight,
  cascading along its pebbled path,
so I joyfully race along my way,
  aching to reach the Sea of Love.

As a lively stream remains ever fresh
  by refusing to stop and pool,
may my restlessness keep me ever alive
  till I am fully alive in you.

 Reflection: *How can we have the time or the desire to gather gold or silver nuggets if we are racing to the Sea? What stream wants to pause and pool when the Ocean is Love — when the magnetic pull is toward complete absorption into the Whole.*

Fear not that you will be damned. Fear, rather, that you will be dammed up. Whether small streams or mighty rivers, only being dammed up prevents them from reaching the sea.

The closer to the ocean, the faster the stream races in breathless bubbling anticipation. Thus, only fools ask, "Why are you in such a hurry to die?"

51

Psalm of the Secret Affair

❧≫ ≪❧

Our secret is divinely delightful,
  this our unknown love affair.
Not married, respectable with rings
  or even sharing the same address,
we meet alone in darkened rooms,
  behind shuttered windows,
making passionate love,
  in the perfume of hiddenness.

Know, O God, that I desire never to end
  this our sweet secret affair —
only my very best of friends suspect
  the great love you and I share.
No proper marriage partner, but a lover
  are you to me, and I to you.
Ever vigilant to leave no clues,
  I speak only occasionally of you.

Not as those who publicly parade
  their affairs with you,
constantly carrying your Book and quoting you,
  more for show than love poured out,
O my Lover, I ceaselessly long to meet you
  at our secret hideaway,
 wishing that our love affair
  will never end.

Reflection: *Jesus was clear in telling us that God loves secret lovers. Those who pray in secret and give alms in secret, he taught, were those God found dearest. The Scriptures speak of a childlike God,*

who finds joy in mature lovers who do secret deeds, for joy in keeping secrets is one of the tests of maturity.

A question to ponder: Whom do you think God finds more delightful, canonized or secret saints?

52

Psalm of the Frightened Lover

O God, let us, you and I,
　　just be friends,
for I fear letting you
　　come too close.

I prefer reverencing you
　　to being romanced
by your love that sweeps
　　even the strongest
off their feet.

Those you love appear insane;
　　your prophets can be a nuisance,
your holy ones seem out of touch
　　and your saviors die in shame.

I fear snakes and cancer,
　　heights and pain,
but most of all I fear you, O God,
　　sweeping me away
in a sea of holy madness.

Reflection: *While pious poetry, song and prayer speak about loving God, when it comes right down to it, most people prefer latex love. Their love of God is mental, or "spiritual" and so keeps them at a safe distance from the disease of divine love. They protect themselves from this affliction that creates the madness of prophets, who not only speak boldly of God but are willing to do so naked on street corners. It's prudent to stay arm's length from such a Lover.*

Those carried out to the sea of divine insanity by the full passionate tide of God's love have names like Francis of Assisi, Joan of Arc, Moses and Mary of Nazareth. Well-advised are those who follow the sage warning: Never go swimming alone, or even wading, in the Great Sea.

T.S. Eliot concludes **Murder in the Cathedral** *with these lines, "Men fear fire and men fear flood and men fear pestilence; but more than anything else they fear the love of God." Those who know the history of the world's holy ones, know only too well the fate of those who allowed God to come too close. They lost their balance and were ripped away from the gravity of their daily life by the stronger, magnetic love of God. Clothes, customs and coins were carelessly cast aside as they were swept out into the ocean of divine love.*

Sensible and balanced, but not blessed, are those who religiously avoid that notorious old flirt named God.

53

Black and Beautiful Psalm
⇒⟫⟪⇐

I am ebony black, but beautiful.
Ah, so beautifully black

am I, your God.

Night is my sacrament,
my sanctuary,
my shrine.
Fear me not.

All things new
are birthed
in me.
Each new day is a seed
planted in the darkness of night.

Death is planting time.
As sunrise is seeded in each sunset,
life is seeded six feet under sod,
in my warm, dark beautiful heart —
so fear not bedding down in me.

 Reflection: *"I am dark, but beautiful," sings the lover in the Song of Songs (1: 5). In the Syrian desert region of Kedar, the nomads' tents were made of black goat hair, and, for desert dwellers, being burnt dark brown by the sun was to be beautifully black. In a poetic and mystical sense, night is Sheik God's great black bridegroom tent.*

The shadow of discrimination that favors white over black and shapes fears of dark strangers also colors our vision of God. Once, black was not only the traditional color for funerals and mourning, but paradoxically also for the most formal and joyous of occasions.

54

Psalm of the Ebony Lover
⋙ ⋘

Ebony God, I love the waves
    of growing purpled blue darkness
that sweep across the earth
    at sunset's last light,
as your shadow embraces me.

I love your ebony darkness,
    in which I, moonlike, float,
 pooled in your womb
    sprinkled with stars.

I love awakening at night,
    drowned in darkness,
smothered with sable kisses,
    wrapped in your embrace.

Candlelight-cast shadows
    are love's dark fingers,
prophets of your presence,
    Beloved Black Death.

Reflection: *"Darkness covered the abyss," is how the Holy Book begins, "while a great wind swept over the waters. Then God said, 'Let there be light'" (Genesis 1: 1-2). Ebony darkness, then, is the primal presence, along with the Spirit Wind sweeping over the bed of waters oozing perfumed juices of life. God comes first, and light comes after darkness. While millenniums of millenniums later holy writers speak of God as light, the primitive presence is darkness.*

Old Gothic cathedrals dwell in darkness, except for faint shafts of stained glass light, and so feel like God houses. Entering into their darkness out of the bright light of day, visitors are inner-urged to remove their shoes, sensing holy dark ground. Stepping back and descending by lantern into old Paleolithic sacred caves whose walls are frescoed by prehistoric Michelangelos is to enter the first God houses. Monastery and cathedral crypts have a similar effect on the pilgrim pray-er.

Today, the absolute darkness of outer space lures astronauts and earth emigrants into the presence of the divine mystery. Darkness also creates a sense of zero gravity, in which even a small candle or flashlight provides a securing measure of gravity. The childhood fear of the dark is perhaps not so much a fear of monsters as it is a prenatal awesome, holy fear of the Divine Dark One.

Human life begins in the darkness of a mother's womb and ends in the darkness of death. Preparing to die begins with learning how to flirt with twilight and continues with romancing the darkness of night. Let the God of Darkness climb into your bed at night, and you will not fear the darkness of death, aware that it is just another womb.

55

Psalm of the Shadow Lover
❧❧❦❦

y Lover is my shadow,
never are we parted,
so nothing do
I fear.

My Lover clings to me,
never am I alone,

so loneliness
is unknown.

If I should walk down an alley
deep-dark with danger,
I know my Lover
is with me.

My Lover is my shadow,
so goodness and joy
shall follow me
always.

 Reflection: *While echoes of Psalm 23, The Lord Is My Shepherd, can be heard in this psalm, it was not a conscious association until after this prayer's birth. It's a companion to the previous psalm, Psalm of the Ebony Lover, and points us back to Christ the Beloved calling himself the Bridegroom.*

Truly intimate with you is your dark shadow, knowing your every secret and clinging to you, naked or dressed, never abandoning you. Even in total darkness, can you be absolutely convinced that your shadow is not next to you, even if you cannot see it?

The human shadow has often been used as a symbol of the negative side of the personality. It can as easily be used as a symbol of the positive, sacred side. Symbolic of the divine presence, it becomes an intimate sacramental shadow.

Watching your shadow, being aware of its ever nearness in the countless activities of your day, even as you climb into bed, can be a prayer of presence. True lovers long to shadow their beloved, loving to linger always at the beloved's side, never to be parted from the beloved, especially in times of great need.

56

The Psalm of Parting
⋙⋘

O Beloved God of Day and Night,
hear my beggar's prayer.
Parting time is so dangerous;
good-byes can be good-alarms,
warning that I may never again
see my beloved in this life.

O Ingenious Creator of all,
for whom nothing is impossible,
with my upraised beggar's cup I plead:
recreate in me your loving image
of a dear and caring shadow.

As your day is followed by night,
soft, dark and beautiful,
and as gentle gray shadows
follow all that lives and moves,
so may my love follow shadow-close
to my departing beloved.

Then ever side-by-side,
at work, at play or in harm's way,
I can shadow my departing beloved
with protecting angelic care,
inseparable from you, my Beloved,
the two of us one loving shadow.

Reflection: *This psalm can be prayed by a wise parent who sends a small child off to school, taking nothing for granted, especially the child's safe return. It can be the prayer of any wise lover, spouse or*

friend, who takes nothing for granted, knowing there is no insurance that the departing beloved will be seen alive again.

Science has yet to develop instruments sensitive enough to detect the presence of love, which clings like a shadow to the beloved. The most advanced technology has yet to create a sensing device capable of measuring the enormous energy created by loving prayer and longing for the presence of the beloved. Thoughts are electric, and when consecrated by prayer they become charged with a cosmic energy that knows no space-time limitations.

This psalm is intended to be a doorway to such loving presence. It can be shrunk down to a single line:

Good-bye, my dear; may God and I be your shadow.

II. Daily Psalms
of Romantic Theology

This section and the previous one might come under the category of romantic theology. Don't be frightened by either of the terms. Theology is simply the study of God. While you may not consider yourself a theologian, would you be reading this book if you were not a student of the Holy? Theologians who have graduate degrees can be of immeasurable assistance in our lives. However, there are homespun theologians who never cease to satisfy their study about the Holy.

The theology of the sacred erotic is found in each of the world's great religions. Some theologians are poetic saints who study God with the heart as well as the mind. Among the long tradition of romantic theologians are the Jewish writers of the Song of Songs and the psalms, Hindu mystics like Mahadeviyakka and Basavana, Islamic saints like Rumi and Kabir, the Christians, Francis of Assisi, St. John of the Cross, St. Theresa of Avila, St. John Climacus and St. Maximus the Confessor of the Orthodox Church tradition of the *Philokalia*, just to name a few.

Love, particularly in its aspect of Eros, has the power to unite things that are totally separated and different. Love makes all things equal, the high and low, the common and the divine. Romantic theology sings not of God as Judge but of God as the Raging Furnace of Love. It celebrates a God of many names who aches to be loved, a God who by the power of that mystical force of love can erase all boundaries that separate.

The troubadours of Southern France from the eleventh to the thirteenth centuries began a Western tradition of love songs that celebrate erotic love. They inspired schools of romantic theology and theologians like St. Bernard of Clairvaux. For some, however, the troubadours were trouble. Because Eros removes the gravity of logic and reason, theologians of morality have often warned against any states of zero gravity created by passion; they have even branded such states as sinful.

From this perspective, dead mystics are the best; the longer they are dead the less radioactive their words and prayers. Overorganized religion cautions us to beware of freethinkers and free-floaters. The latter are lovers of God who defy solemn gravity and so drift effortlessly up and over the walls of religion. They are characterized by crystal clear eyes, and are the God-struck and soul-singed.

A soon-approaching tomorrow will call out for volunteers to emigrate into space. Free-floaters can step confidently forward to emigrate from Earth to the New Earth in space. Those who have floated freely in God's space will be certified as safe, since they will not be carriers of this planet's ancient plague, the deadly virus of religious superiority.

In that free-floating spirit that seeks to breathe only the breath of God, the psalms in this section celebrate human love as one with divine love.

57

A Psalm of Falling in Love
-»>«<-

O Divine Lover, come to my aid;
 O God, come to my assistance.
For I have fallen in love,
  and gravity is on vacation.
I'm floating on air,
  carefree as a school-free child,

joyful as a lottery winner,
>since gravity's rug has been pulled
from under my feet.

Do not come to rescue me,
>my ever youthful Beloved.
Come and celebrate with me
>my free-fall somersaulting
into the Promised Land
>flowing with milk and honey.

Come and dance with me
>to the tapping tango
of my new love affair;
>come, levitate with me,
my head high among the stars.

O God, come not to rescue me;
>rather, come celebrate with me,
for by this falling in love,
>I've fallen into you.

 Reflection: *The intoxicating power of love that defies gravity was expressed in a song from the musical* **My Fair Lady**: *"I have often walked on these streets before, but the pavement always stayed beneath my feet before." Falling in love is usually considered the affliction of the young, yet ageless is this acrobatic trick practiced by those of all ages. Love's zero-gravitational field defies age.*

If you feel you have grown beyond such flights of fancy, frequently practice this self-blinding exercise: Look at something you love or even something as common as the view from your window, then close your eyes for a minute or two. In the blackness of self-blindness, pretend that what you saw has been taken away, as has your sight. Then open your eyes and drink in with great gratitude the sight before you — and fall in love with it.

Falling in love is the secret entrance to the Fountain of Youth. To find it you need only to make temporarily uncommon and absent what is usually commonplace to you. Aging is reversed in proportion to the amount of time spent in cultivating and celebrating the state of falling in love.

58

The Psalm of Forever
➤➤➤ ‹‹‹

orever is a holy word
    I've stolen from God's vocabulary
that I dare to utter
    when speaking of my love for you.

From the ten thousand names of God,
    with lips trembling in fear,
I have chosen Forever
    to sing of my love for you.

Idolatry — to make human love divine
    and put it on par with God.
No, not idolatry, but identity,
    for love and God are one
when love longs to be Forever.

O You who never created love,
    but *are* Love, and Love-Forever,
gift me with Your sacred heart
    to love You, and my beloved,
Forever, Forever.

Reflection: *With holy fear and trembling, lovers say they will love each other forever. They dare, with their hair standing on end in fear, to use the name of God as a pledge that their love will withstand anything that might drag them apart, even death.*

From the beginning, God wedded human love and God-love together as one and the same — even when human loving falls short of forever. Gratefully, human love is awakened to its Godhood whenever such love struggles to be forever.

The tree of love can withstand all storms, droughts and disasters when its roots are entwined around the God-Stone at the center of the Earth. Love's zero gravity is made stable by being thus grounded in Ground Zero. Each time "Forever" is whispered in the darkness, it sends the roots of love racing to encircle more tightly the Sacred Stone.

So anchored in Love, our loves can withstand the dry desert winds of routine, the twisting tornadoes of emotional differences, infidelity and workaday chaos.

Forever — let us say it slowly, say it full of meaning, say it as one of the holy names of God.

This and many of the psalms in this chapter are addressed to a human beloved rather than to God. Yet they are still prayers, as they speak of how mutual human love is the very presence of God.

59

The Magnet of Love Psalm
⋙⋘

As a magnet sucks a nail
    unto its very self;
as the needle of a compass
    swings unchecked

toward magnetic North,
  so I am drawn to you.

Drawn magnetically
  are my eyes to your face.
Your beauty holds me
  bound tightly,
a captive of the magnetizing love
  I feel for you.

Beauty, the ancients said,
  is what pleases us,
and, my beloved, you please me
  more than anyone or anything
that I have ever known.

May neither the red rust of time
  nor conflict's clawhammer
ever cause the magnet of our love
  to lose its power
to keep us together forever.

 Reflection: *The art of long-lasting love begins with what attracts us to another person. It seems that what is viewed as beautiful is determined by some previously formed inner design coded in our human makeup. As magical as it is for an iron nail to be drawn to a magnet, even more magical is human attraction. What attracts one fails to do so for another.*

The pleasing attraction begins when someone fits this primal inner pattern. For love to be long lasting, it must be purified by mutual sacrifice and communion with Love itself, for all magnetic fields shift. The magnetic north pole which attracts the needle of a compass is not stationary, but moves in an elliptical pattern. Ancient monuments that were once aligned with the North Star are now out of alignment. This shift continues today, and 2,000 years from now Earth's North Star will shift from the present star

to Alpha Cephei.

When purified by a spirit of self-sacrifice and perpetual pardoning, the magnet of love moves from an attraction to physical, external beauty to an attraction to awesome inner beauty. The magnet power binding two people as one shifts toward the beauty of inner qualities like loyalty, tenderness, companionship, compassion, shared history and delight in the differences that harmonize instead of divide.

60

The Psalm of Aged Arousal
⇛⇚

No miracles do I need,
  no wonders to behold,
to continue to love you,
  my beloved.

I find my delight in daily,
  seemingly drab companionship,
simply sitting next to you
  in our silent conversations.

I'm aroused by your loving loyalty,
  my heart pounding
in anticipation of nothing new,
  except my being next to you.

I sensually and lovingly finger
  my rosary beads of shared memories,
massaging and caressing them
  like a youthful lover's body.

Reflection: *That God is love is a divine, not a human, definition. The more Godlike human love becomes, the more enduring and eternal it grows. In all loving, romance must be a fire daily enkindled in the hearth of the heart. Love needs to daily gather kindling to feed the fire. For routine is the rust that corrodes the magnetic power of love. Be diligent to scrape that rust off your loves.*

As the magnetic pole of human love shifts with time, so does the mystical magnetic pole of love for God. What drew you to God at one age is not what draws you at another time in your life. As aged human lovers can be tempted to long for the steamy-hot passions of youth and mistake the absence of flaming desire for the departure of love, so too with holy lovers.

As old lovers can be exchanged for younger ones who are more capable of fitting a primal pattern of beauty, so new, more "exiting" gods can become attractive. Resist revivalists who try to sell you some new lover-God with their fire-and-smoke miracles. Instead, find delight and seasoned passion in the deep, quiet, loving companionship of your faithful, enduring loves.

61

The Goodbye-Hello Psalm

Beloved, we stand at the door,
    poised to say an echoing good-bye,
a parting invested with mystical powers
    never to die on the wind.

God, who has no end or beginning,
    is sandwiched in the word Good-bye.

So, may the good in my good-bye
  roll endlessly in space and time.

As I say "good-bye, good-bye, good-bye,"
  I tie an echo tail of love
to you, my beloved, until full-circle
  it comes round to "hello, hello, hello"
  and "welcome home."

 Reflection: *Can true lovers ever really part and depart from one another? For those whom love has made — and is still making — one, departing is smoke-and-mirrors magic, a mirage at a doorstep or airport separation. Even Death the Butcher cannot chop in two the flesh fused as one by love's communion.*

The Butcher Shop of Death is located on every corner in the town called Daily-life. Don't close your eyes as you pass it by; rather, let it remind you how to properly say good-bye. Daily tie a sacred string of good-byes to departing loved ones to hold them devotion-bound till your string, yo-yo-like, returns with hellos and welcome homes. Daily parting with such sacred strings can make even the final good-bye at the door of death a short string of hello, hello, hello that ties us together across the mystery of coming Home.

The practical life and the spiritual life are one, so consider attaching such a string to your prayers. Traditionally, prayer and worship end with a dead and flat amen. Sung, shouted or spoken, amen signals the curtain-closing of a holy time. Sometimes it's hard to determine whether amen is a profession of faith or a sigh of relief that we've encountered God and lived to escape. So think about concluding your personal prayers with a sacred string of good-byes, which can circle back again into hellos and so create a never-ending prayer.

62

Psalm of a Rewounded Lover

I fear my wound has healed
    with the passing of time,
and so no longer bleeds red
    like new wine.

Unasked-for healing,
    working days and nights
over years and years,
    has scabbed shut my open wound.

Now I try to pick at
    my hard-crusted lover's scab
so I can again feel the ache
    of joyous love.

Ever-wounded, I long to live
    all my days,
limping, feverish, sick
    with love for you.

Reflection: Romantic love is a prairie fire, wind-blown and impossible to extinguish, except by the dripping waters of time. Time douses the flames of such love which might easily withstand the fire extinguishers of common sense and logic.

Romance is the first stage in the evolution of loving that rips through life like a destructive tornado. All romance wounds us, yet time heals all wounds. There are some wounds, however, that need to be kept open, that need to be picked at daily with the fingernail of fondness.

Young lovers walk with hands glued together, lest some jealous god springs out and robs them of each other. Young lovers also limp like a pair in a three-legged race, since they can no longer walk alone. Young lovers of any age have a wound in their chest, for their hearts have been broken into. Music and perfume, joy and delight pour out of those wounds, yet time heals all wounds.

Wise lovers ask the Holy Spirit, the Finger of God, to pick away at the scabs of youthful loves and friendships and to peel back the brown-crusted scab grown hard over the sacred wound in the heart.

63

The Neighbor Psalm

I love you, my known and unknown lover,
with all the passion I can arouse.
I love you, whoever you are,
you, who at this moment
are here next to me,
and who are
Neighbor.

I love you, you whose body is near mine;
with a longing heart I love you
who are now so very close
and yet so very distant,
so different from me;
yet you are my
Neighbor.

I love you with my smile and warm greeting,
and with my helping hand of love,

for with great joy I do recognize
even in your clever disguise
the face of my Beloved
in yours, my
Neighbor.

 Reflection: *The greatest call of God is "Love me!" We can hardly name it a law or commandment, for how can anyone command love? God is unashamedly, longingly direct: "Love me!" God speaks the secret* language of every lover, secret because those two words are so difficult to utter yet linger unspoken on all lips.

In response, the human lover, who can love only what can be embraced, cries out, "How, for God's sake?" God knows our problem and replies, "It's easy, love whomever is next to you: stranger–friend–enemy–family–alien–associate–foreigner–old–young–black–red–white–yellow–ugly–able–disabled–beautiful–poor–angry–rich–in-a-hurry–drunk–lonely–needy–Neighbor.

Each moment, each encounter with our neighbor is an invitation to make love. More than just someone who lives next door, in Hebrew and Greek **neighbor** *implies whoever happens to be next to you. Finding such passionate loving of strangers, foreigners or enemies too much for the heart to stomach, religious lawyers fenced in* **neighbor**, *restricting it to those of the neighborhood of one's own clan, religion and country. Yet God has no eyes for such artificial boundary lines.*

Nothing so radically changes our day more than falling in love with whomever is next to us. This last psalm of the chapter speaks of the greatest mastery of loving and challenges each of us who say we love God.

Chapter 4
New Testament Psalms

I. Disciple Psalms

 The Psalms attributed to King David in the First Testament hold a significant and beloved place among the books of the Bible. Because there are so many fewer song-poems in the Second Testament, the next two chapters of this book are devoted to New Testament psalm-prayers.

The preceding chapter on devotional psalms is an ideal preface to this one because devotion should flow out into deeds. Jesus called his disciples to devotion in loving God with all their hearts and loving God in their neighbor. By baptism they were called not simply to perform good works but to do them inspired by and filled with love. As residents of the reign of God which has already arrived, disciples are always emigrating to that new land — while still living in the old.

The Master never made mystical ecstasy important, nor did he promise visions or altered states of consciousness to his followers. Yet ecstasy's original meaning was to be "out of place" or to be "out of one's senses." Such a state is another expression of zero gravity and could be called E-G, *ecstasy gravity.* Being faithful to the deeds to which Jesus called his disciples requires E-G, being out of ourselves and sometimes outside the gravity field of common sense.

Zero gravity comes in stages, in ever expanding degrees. Each stage causes the previous sense of stable grounding of daily life to be turned upside down. Certainly Jesus' liberation of his followers from the religious gravity (R-G) of the sacrifices of the temple in Jerusalem and their daily religious obligations was a disorienting experience. Following him and embracing his teachings must have caused his disciples to lose the secure footing of their religious tradition and to find themselves in joyful free-floating freedom, even if it was also unsettling.

The psalms in these next two chapters are psalms for the new gravity field created when the arrival of the promise made long ago to Abraham and Sara suddenly appeared in the person of Jesus. They celebrate the good news of Jesus' new gravitational field of poverty of spirit, service and discipleship. These psalms are intended to help us adapt and align ourselves to the New Testament's zero gravity.

64

The Disciple's Creed
⇒⟫⟪⇐

I believe in God, the Almighty,
    creator of heaven and earth.
I believe in Jesus the Christ,
    God's only Son and my Lord.
He was conceived by the power of the Holy Spirit
    and was born of the Virgin Mary.

He was baptized in water and the Holy Spirit,
    then went about announcing to all
    that the reign of God had arrived.

He associated with the lowly and poor,
    eating with sinners and outcasts
    and forgiving their sins with compassion.
He called his disciples
    to daily take up their crosses and follow him,
    denying their very selves, reforming their lives.
His disciples were to pray constantly
    and to forgive each other without end.
Jesus gave only one commandment:
    to love God with all our heart, mind and body,
    and to love our neighbors as ourselves.
At table, the night before his death,
    he gave away his body and blood to redeem all
    in a meal of his new covenant,
    a meal to be kept by his disciples in memory of him.

He suffered under Pontius Pilate,
    was crucified, died and was buried.
He descended to the dead;
    on the third day he was raised up.
He ascended into heaven
    and is seated at the right hand of God.
He will come again
    to judge the living and the dead.

I believe in the Holy Spirit,
    the holy, catholic Church,
    the communion of saints,
    the forgiveness of sins,
    the resurrection of the body,
    and the life everlasting. Amen.

 Reflection: *There are two great Christian creeds, the Nicean Creed and the Apostles' Creed. The first was composed at the Council of Nicea in 325 and expanded at the First Council of Constantinople in*

381. The Apostles' Creed, according to legend, was composed by the twelve apostles, yet the earliest reference to it as a formulated statement goes back only to an eighth century letter by St. Ambrose. Both these creeds appear to have their source in the responses made by those being baptized in the early church as a summary of their faith.

Robert Funk, a scripture scholar, calls the Apostles' Creed a "donut creed" since it has a gaping hole in the middle. The creed immediately skips from Jesus being born of the Virgin Mary to his being crucified by Pontius Pilate. The above Disciple's Creed attempts to fill in some of the gap. It is also intended to be an energizing daily profession of faith, reminding us what is required to be a disciple of Jesus.

Simply following church regulations to the letter and believing in a creed are the signs of a minimal rather than a living faith. Yet creeds can be prayers of faith that powerfully influence the deeds of daily life. They can help us follow the radical lifestyle of our Lord, Master and Teacher, Jesus, who said, "Come, follow me."

65

Mother Mary's Magnificent Psalm
-≫ ≪-

My motherly soul proclaims
the greatness of our Lord.
My spirit rejoices in my savior God,
for God will sweep away
the gravity of high places,
causing the great ones to come tumbling down
to the lowest places.

God will make the arrogant and proud of heart look silly
as they turn head over heels, bottoms up.

Then the poor and untouchables
  will shoot up to the top,
passing the rich plunging downward.

God's magnetic new reign
  will reverse the gravity of the world's gravy train,
causing the fat and rich to be thrown off
  as the starving hungry fill to overflowing
every feasting car of this new train.

For this coming great reign
  my soul rejoices to the heavens
in God who is truly our savior.

 Reflection: *The promise made to Abraham, Sara and their countless descendents through Christ was kept by the Promise Maker. Yet, the fullness of it still remains the daily task of the promise workers, those to whom God has entrusted the divine work. By our baptism into Christ, each of us shares in that responsibility. It is by deeds drenched in devotion that we take that responsibility seriously, making the new reign of God as present as possible wherever possible. The age of God is constantly moving forward, and so each of us is continuously called to pray and work to fulfill the reign of God in ourselves and our world.*

Yet, to be a part of God's new world is no grim, grit-your-teeth duty. Rather, it is to be a joyful, ecstatic delight, as it was for Mother Mary, the first disciple of the Good News. It is essential to have a personal romantic theology — as we reflected upon in the last chapter — in order to make our deeds magnificently joyful.

Before Jesus would announce the good news that God's reign had already come, his mother Mary sang her great song of a world turned upside down. It was a magnificent psalm by a pregnant prophet-mother of the coming age of zero gravity. It is the overture to the other psalm-songs in this chapter.

66

Psalm of the Name of the Holy Power
⋙⋘

Help me, my God,
  whenever I begin a new task,
    when stumped with a problem,
    when stalled in my work,
    when faced with weakness,
        to pray
In the name of the Father and of the Son
    and of the Holy Power.

I call upon the Holy Power of Kindness
    when I am tempted to be rude.
I call upon the name of God's Powerful Strength
    when I am tempted to be weak.
I call upon the name of God's Great Creativity
    when I am tempted to copy
    or to fall back upon a tired, old solution.

For great is the name of the Holy Power,
    rushing like a whirlwind
to shape the primal chaos into order,
    creating life throughout the universe.

Powerful beyond all the powers of Earth
    is the fire of God's Spirit,
whose flaming heat forges heroes and heroines
    out of timid, hiding cowards,
boiling listless, lukewarm spirits
    into churning steam engines of energy.

In the name of the creative Holy Power,
    I pray:
Come! Amen.

Reflection: *The Holy Spirit composed the magnificent psalm of Mary, and the Spirit's fingers played the harp of her heart as she sang it. The same Spirit kissed into life the child-seed in her womb, and would return for a more fiery passionate embrace later in her son's life.*

After Jesus was baptized in the waters of the Jordan and in the power of the Holy Spirit, his life was dramatically set aflame. For almost thirty years prior to that nothing worth writing about seems to have happened to Jesus of Galilee. Then he underwent the baptism of John, in which the Holy Power of God descended in full Spirit upon him. At this point, the gravity of his hometown life was reduced to zero, and he became the Messenger-Singer of God's new era.

This psalm to the Spirit of God sets the tone for the following disciple-hinge psalm since the Spirit that first filled Jesus was also promised by the Master as his gift to all his disciples. Whenever you pray this psalm, wear your fireproof suit and tie yourself firmly to the doorpost of your home, lest the Wind of God also send you off as a messenger. (Additional psalms to the Spirit are found in Chapter 5.)

67

The Hinge Psalm
⇒》《⇐

IF you are following your Master,
    you can abandon your business
and walk away from your fishing nets and boats —
    with confidence — like a chapter closed.

IF you are following your Beloved,
　　you can easily rise from your desk
and leave the counting of coins,
　　worrying not about what you will do next.

IF you are carefree as little sparrows
　　and enjoy the fashions of field lilies,
you can walk away from your job and responsibilities,
　　not worrying about tomorrow's needs.

IF you love your Beloved Master
　　more than father, friend, fortune and family,
more than mother, money and mutual funds,
　　then you will be given a hundredfold
of all these in this life and in Life-without-end.

The door of your destiny hangs
　　on the simple, single hinge of IF.

Reflection: *"No Job Security" is the frightening sign hanging over our times. Downsized or right-sized, by whatever name, countless hard-working, dedicated employees daily find their jobs have disappeared. Our job provides a field of gravity; its grounding flows from its regular schedule and daily routine. It also provides a stabilizing community, a workday family, a clan to which one belongs. Like the ancient tribal clan, our job also can provide care in sickness and other social benefits. Thus, to lose one's job is to be deported as an unwilling emigrant to a fearful foreign colony, the Isle of the Idle, the Devil's Island of the Unemployed.*

Those deported to this most feared place are typically anxious about their tomorrows, feeling that their future depends only on their own efforts. IF, however, they are following the Master and Beloved, they need not be anxious about what they will eat or wear, or where they will work next.

"What madness!" cry out practical folk. "You've got to be

feebleminded if you lose your job and are not worried sick about yourself and your family." Yet IF you are not feebleminded, but rather are firm-minded because of your faith in the promise of Jesus, you can rejoice in your state of zero gravity. You might even declare your state of unemployment to be a surprise vacation — like a halftime intermission, an opportunity to stand up, take a break and relax.

IF, IF . . . .

68

Psalm of a Mystical Blind Lover
⋙⋘

O Jesus of Galilee — whose face drew lovers
    as honey draws flies — help this blind "fly."
St. Paul was thrown from his horse,
    blinded by a glorious bright vision of you.
Saints and mystics in every century
    have had similar visions of you and your mother.
Such visions continue to this very day.

O Beloved Master, alas, I too am blind,
    yet I long to be graced by a vision of you.
Sadly, I confess to not having seen a single one,
    whether on a road or in a time of prayer.
Help me, your blind disciple, who longs for,
    yet fears, such divine visitations,
for they may turn my comfortable world upside down.

Cure me of my desire for mystic visions
    and so open my eyes to see you

in every beautiful flower, sunset, woman or man,
  God's glory enfleshed in beauty.
Let my eyes see your glory in oozing pain,
  in every ugly, sick, disfigured, dying body
and in all throwaway humans and "freaks" of nature,
  because God's glory is truly visible
in every ugliness as well as every beauty.

Heal my deaf eyes, as well, Beloved Master,
  so I can hear your whisper in what I see,
calling upon me to love you in everything that is.

 Reflection: *Holiness is attributed to those persons who are said to have seen the extraordinary, the mystical. Starving for the rare bread of the parapsychological, crowds flock around visionaries, hoping to catch a small glimpse of heaven visiting earth.*

Jesus of Galilee invited those who were vision-challenged to be his friends and to follow him. Those who did were promised the healing gift of seeing visions. Jesus' healing formula for his blind friends was to follow him and to anoint their eyes with love; then they would see Christ in everyone. Those who desire any other kind of mystical vision are advised to take note of the warning label below.

Caution:

Mystical visions can cause you to be thrown off your high horse, even if you are not on one. You may suffer a severe loss of gravity, as your world and everything in it, including your religion, are turned upside down. **Final Warning:** *Visions may lead to crucifixions.*

69

A Psalm of Seeing God
⇥⇤

God, the Imageless,
created us
in the divine image.
Everything, then,
is the image of God.

As every author,
we are told,
reveals himself
in his words,
is not God imaged, then,
in you?

Creation,
from a blade of grass
to oceans and galaxies,
is a volume
of images of God.

Those with eyes to see
need no
God picture books,
no mystic visions
of the No-Image One.

Reflection: *Jesus must have been initiated into Jewish mysticism since his words reflect an essential ingredient of its way of seeing: the importance of rediscovering God in all aspects of human life. Jesus so closely identified himself with God that to see him was to see God. He pushed the frontiers of this communion to the point*

where all who loved him and were one with him also shared in his holy communion.

Jesus is called the Word of God made flesh. The first words of God were made flesh in creation. God spoke, and in a flash the sun appeared, then the moon and stars, the crickets and ants, and all creation. With this image of creation clearly in focus, Jewish mystical spirituality saw all words, especially words of prayer, as extremely important vehicles to go to God.

Look with great reverence upon all of God's words made flesh — words of flesh, fur, fin and feather — and use them as vehicles to return to the Source.

70

The Magician Giver Psalm

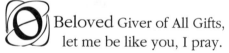

O Beloved Giver of All Gifts,
    let me be like you, I pray.

Give me the skilled hands of a magician,
    clever in sleight of hand,
so I can give a gift with my right hand,
    unseen and unknown to my left.

By practice may I perfect this secret art
    in every corner of my life,
in caring for the poor at home and afar,
    and so become a phantom giver.

Train me to be so crafty and clever
    with my sleight-of-hand charity
that not even you, my God, will see it,
    for then my gifts will be like yours.

Reflection: *Matthew (6: 3) records the Master's magical requirements for giving alms, since all charity can be dangerous to the soul. The Master challenged his disciples to be magicians so skilled as to even fool themselves: "When you give gifts of charity, do so secretly so that your left hand does not know what the right is doing."*

What have you gained if you give away all your money to the poor, but lose your soul in the process by holding a press conference to announce your great charity? Being photographed signing charity checks, having your name emblazoned on bronze plaques or giving alms while your right hand is shaking your left in congratulations — all these are activities of magicless disciples. Such un-clever and acclaim-hungry followers are sadly ignorant of God's passionate love of secrecy.

Blessed are you who in giving gifts not only fool yourselves but even try to fool God! Blessed are you, for you will know the zero gravity of the Gospel. You will taste the ecstatic, drunken joy of a secret, passionate kiss from God.

71

The Furnace Psalm
⋙⋘

ear my cry, O Master Goldsmith,
   who has recast me in your furnace,
causing me to undergo the searing, cleansing fire
      of your alchemy of suffering.
Having endured the trial, all aglow,
      I've come forth as gold.

My suffering now forgotten,
      I shine like the sun, precious as a gem.

O God, will you mold me now
　　into your golden throne of heaven
or fashion me into your royal crown
　　to shine in goldenly beauty?

In your mercy, do not stamp me now,
　　into a rare golden coin of your realm,
one richly imprinted with your sacred seal,
　　for I fear I will be greedily fingered
by religious prostitutes and pious merchants of the holy
　　or by gamblers who want to win you cheaply,
without sweating in the spirit and in hard work.

Once again, pour me back, I pray, O God,
　　into your furnace of purifying love,
there, Divine Alchemist, to melt away from me
　　all but the purest gold of love.
Then, dear God, mold me
　　into the commonest coin of your realm.

 Reflection: *To have passed through God's furnace of suffering and come forth as godly gold, pure and unpolluted, seems the final achievement. The suffering smelting process has removed the dross, the impurities, from the ore. Now the gold can be fashioned into a wedding ring, a chalice, a tabernacle or some other beautiful creation of the jeweler's craft.*

For true saints, another smelting is needed, in which golden halos are recycled in heaven's forge to become golden bed pans or golden coins for beggars' cups. They willingly suffer the unique zero gravity of having reached their "final stage" of refinement, only to see the need to be recycled again — and again.

True saints are God's golden pennies who are shamelessly handled by those eager to exploit them, those who seek to manipulate them for their own selfish needs. These pennies from heaven do not try to judge the motives of those who use them,

leaving that only to God. Even though already purified by their
suffering, they seek the zero gravity of being put to common use.

72

Psalm of the Road
✦≫≪✦

My Beautiful Friend,
you are the Map, but more;
you are also the Road and the Way!

You are the Lover's Lane
with unknown twists,
with turns round every bend.

As I travel with you, my Beloved,
I know the feel of the bumps in the road
as well as the pain of being treaded upon
by careless or self-serving life-travelers.

Yet, my heart explodes
with joy ecstatic,
simply knowing I am a cobblestone
of you, the Way.

Reflection: *Jesus called himself the Way. Aware*
of love's unity, he also said that every lover and he
were one. So interconnected would they be that
whatever was done to even the most outcast of his
lovers would be done directly to him.

Because of that amazing divine unity, each of us also can say,
"I am the Way." A true lover rejoices in being even the most seemingly
insignificant cobblestone among countless others, unnoticed by

those taking another life path and even unseen by travelers hurrying along the Way with their vision fixed forward only on God.

We can find this to be happily humbling and ecstatically joyful good news. For the exuberant joy of the zero gravity of the Gospel takes the air out of grave self-importance. In this zero gravity we can rejoice even at being walked over, trodden upon and treaded smooth because we realize that we are part of the Holy Highway of Love.

73

Psalm of God's Good Time

-≫≪-

Divine Friend, I feel sorry
for those whose clocks
have faces that are circled
with terrible things
rather than twelve numbers.

I pray for those who
measure time by misfortunes,
their miseries the minutes
ticked off with groans
that life is so painful.

In their hourglass of life
each grain of sand is a sorrow,
trickling trials piling up,
making mountains of miseries
from molehills of sad sand.

May I keep your good time, O God:

all my clocks measuring life
only by counting your rich blessings,
hour by hour, your gifts galore,
making twice as long
a lifetime ticking with thanksgiving.

 Reflection: *Saint Paul proclaimed the need to give thanks always and for everything. Regardless of the symbols or numbers printed on the face of your wristwatch or clock, to keep time according to God's good time is to know what time it is: It is time to give thanks.*

B.C., Before Clocks, was a time kept by sun and stars. Our age is surrounded by clocks who are slave drivers; their hands whip us to keep us running in a hurry. To some degree, we are victims of time's destiny and our individual circumstances, our conflicts and problems that measure out our existence. Yet to some degree, our slavery to the clock is self-imposed. Wanting to control our lives and our destinies, we crowd our schedules. When we can't make things work, the clock squeezes us mercilessly, and we define life in terms of delays, interruptions and problems.

Fortunate are those who have emigrated to the Promised Land of Gratitude, for they have crossed the border into the paradise of zero gravity. While to others they may seem not to have gone anywhere — living in the same house and working at the same job — they live in a different time zone. They are freed of grave attitudes, for they have placed their lives in God's hands, not in the tyrant-clock's hands. They measure life and time by being grateful, regardless of whether the situation is pleasant or unpleasant, problem-free or problem-filled. Such grateful living makes us gravity-free, buoyed only by God's blessings and love.

"Watch carefully how you live, and don't be foolish," the writer of Ephesians says, "giving thanks always and for everything" (Ephesians 5: 15-20). Watching your watch carefully — marking time with gratitude — is the key to not living foolishly. May your watch be an instrument for counting your blessings.

74

Psalm of a Beggar at God's Door

(This psalm can be accompanied by knocking.)

Hear me, O God, I stand at your door.
    (knock, knock, knock)

A beggar, friend and lover stands
    waiting at your door.
I come to you with my list of needs,
    doing as I was told.
Hear the knocking of your beloved
    begging at your door.

(knock, knock, knock)

I confess that it is not you, my God,
    who closes shut your door.
Forgive my rudeness, Divine Beloved,
    for often slamming it in your face.
Now, with a prayerful closed fist
    I strike my breast, my heart.
I'm sorry that I often come not to make love
    but only when I'm in some special need.

(knock, knock, knock)

Hear me as I now knock at your door;
    open wide to me your heart,
for now, as a beggar at your door,
    I plead for my needs: *(list here your petitions)* .

(knock, knock, knock)

With confidence I knock in prayer,
    for it was your son Jesus
who taught me this trick of tapping
    and promised you would always open
to answer those at your door.

Holy *(knock)*, Holy *(knock)*, Holy *(knock)*.

Reflection: *Jesus promised his disciples that if they knock, God will open the door with gifts for the asking. Naturally, God is eager to have an ever opened door, wanting to anticipate our every need. For God is like a lover who never needs to be asked what gift the beloved desires.*

Although God doesn't need to be asked, our knocking in prayer reminds us of our relationship with God; it strengthens the bonds of love, as we take neither our needs nor God for granted. Knocking in prayer also reminds us that it is we who so often close the door to God. We shut the door by being too busy opening the doors to success. We block the door by being too well fed and too well dressed.

Finally, knocking is a good musical accompaniment to prayer. It helps tune our ears, and if our ears are attuned we can hear God's response to our knocking: "Come in, my beloved, it isn't locked."

75

The Doorkeeper's Psalm
➔➤➤ ⇇⇇⇇

Help Wanted: *Doorkeeper. Male or female. Must be courteous, dignified and congenial. Uniform with large gold buttons and gold braid, along with a tall black silk hat, is provided. Apply at the servant's entrance of the Grand Hotel.*

Divine Beloved, you whose simplest residence
    is always a grand hotel,
I would love to apply for the full-time position
    of being the keeper of the door to you.

And, yes, O God, I do have some experience
   to recommend me for the job.

For those who have come wanting to see you,
   I've opened many a door:
The old woman so hungry for attention,
   I held the door open for an hour
just prayerfully, reverently, listening to her story.

For my neighbor who came heavily burdened
   with her list of many woes for you to hear,
I held the door open, and my ears and heart as well.

I've opened many doors for those who've come in need
   on the street, in a letter, on a plane, in bed.
I've also opened doors by being blind to rudeness,
   and by forgiving an offense.

Oh, my past certainly isn't that of some great saint;
   I've made my share of mistakes and sins.
Yet I ask you not to let those parts of my past
   cloud my resume,
for, truly, my *vitae* does not adequately qualify me
   to be in your employ.
So I come to the servant's entrance of your grand hotel,
   asking you to look only at my present longing,
my desire to work for you
   as your humble keeper of the door.

 Reflection: *Holy Orders began as a series of ordinations to various orders or steps to the priesthood. The first order was that of porter, keeper of the door. The door the porters kept lead to the place of the Eucharist, the place of holy communion.*

By baptism, each disciple, female or male, is ordained to be drained. The fundamental way to be drained is in the service of opening doors for those coming to God, even if they are not actually

looking for God. Many are seeking places with names like comfort,
encouragement, understanding, company — and all the other
addresses of Love.

After proper prayer and reflection, even if you lack good
references, consider asking God to ordain you to the order of
doorkeeper. All those interested, be they sinners or saints, should
come around to the servant's entrance of the Grand Hotel to apply
for employment/ordination.

76

The Temple Custodian's Psalm
⇒⟫⟪⇐

God of Hosts, when your Holy Temple in Jerusalem
was leveled to the ground,
leaving not a stone left upon a stone,
	did the sky-blue floor of heaven
bounce beneath your joyful, dancing feet?

When your no-entry, holy of holies home
	was flattened to the earth,
did the roaring of your laughter shatter
	the great polar ice glaciers
into a hundred billion diamond crystals?

Be honest with me, O God of the Truth
	and nothing but the Truth.
Confirm for me my suspicion
	that you loved dwelling in Old Moses' traveling tent,
that you were ecstatic to be free again, at last.

"Let us go up to the house of God,"

once sang Zion's temple pilgrims.
"Let us not *go* but *be* in God's house,"
now sing we priestly caretakers
of your cosmic holy of holies house.

 Reflection: *Priesthood began as custodial work.*
The temples required janitors ordained to the sacred
duty of housekeeping the houses of the gods.

With the announcement of Jesus that God's
temple had exploded outward to include all the Earth and beyond,
ecology became, for those who know where they live, a priestly duty.
Each of us is now a priestly caretaker of God's holy shrine, Earth.

Woe to those priestly custodians who litter God's sacred space
with trash. Woe to those emigrating holy caretakers who someday
will go to outer space and leave behind a depleted holy land,
polluted holy pools and rivers, and unbreathable temple air.

Will such careless priestly caretakers find mercy for their
woeful housekeeping of the temple of Earth?

Each time you pick up a piece of trash along the road, say to
yourself, "Holy, holy, holy is the house of God."

77

Psalm of the Secret Obedient Disciples
➜➤➤ ⫷⫷⫷

The Beloved Master said,
"This is my body,
this is my blood;
do this in memory of me."
"This is my body, this is my blood,"

once was spoken by all disciples
obedient to the Master's last request.
Yet after a thousand years,
"This is my body, this is my blood,"
became clergy copyrighted.

Let those with ears hear:
Gray clouds heavy with rain that weep,
"This is my body, this is my blood."
Let those with ears hear
the self-consuming sun say,
"This is my body, this is my blood."

Listen carefully, all, to hear:
Salmon, corn and cow, grape and goat say,
"This is my body, this is my blood."
And lovers abed under a full moon moan,
"This is my body, this is my blood."

Listen carefully, all, and hear:
A loving mother to her newborn silently says,
"This is my body, this is my blood."
At the diversity of Emmaus meals,
may the Master's disciples not fear to say,
"This is my body, this is my blood."

 Reflection: *Jesus, who commanded the keeping of the one law of love of God and neighbor, also clearly commanded his disciples at the Last Supper, "Do this in memory of me." The keeping of that memory is at the heart and soul of the community of his followers. For two millenniums the church-community has kept this mystical commandment of its dying lover.*

However, are those who are entrusted with this commission obedient disciples or copyright pirates? Jesus' words that enshrine the memory are indeed copyrighted today — that is, they are

*restricted to the clergy — but that has not always been the case.
For a good millennium, some scholars claim, the keeping of the
Memory was not the exclusive right of a few. That millennium
established a long tradition of a universal right, a right to which
obedient disciples perhaps ought now to return.*

78

"Do This in Memory of Me" Psalm

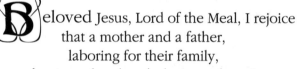

eloved Jesus, Lord of the Meal, I rejoice
  that a mother and a father,
    laboring for their family,
  begin and end each day's work saying,
  "This is my body, this is my blood."

An adult child nursing a sick elderly parent
  with compassion and patient care says,
    "This is my body, this is my blood."

A volunteer giving time to a needy cause
  without thanks or acknowledgment says,
    "This is my body, this is my blood."

A preacher, with prayerful study, preparing a homily
  that no one may remember or be moved by, says,
    "This is my body, this is my blood."

A singer forgetting self and the audience,
  making love out of the music, says,
    "This is my body, this is my blood.

Artist or teacher, dancer or doctor,

auto mechanic or office worker,
attending to each detail of their work
with full-hearted involvement, proclaim,
"This is my body, this is my blood."

Ten thousand thousand consecrations occur daily,
as all heaven's angels chime in,
"Holy, holy, holy,"
to the thunderous praise
of a thousand silent silver bells.
Listen. Listen.

 Reflection: *Some theologians as late as the twelfth century held that there was no necessary connection between the consecration of bread and wine into Christ's Body and Blood and sacramental ordination. Gary Macy, chairman of the theology department of the University of San Diego and a scholar of the medieval period, discovered that the first document making a distinction between laity and ritually ordained clergy didn't appear until the Fourth Lateran Council of 1215.*

To frequently make a gift of yourself in loving compassionate service is being faithful to Jesus, keeping the memory of his gift alive and doing what he did. While his gift-words are officially restricted to the ordained clergy today, Jesus' last request on the night before he died was restricted to neither time nor place, person nor circumstance. We all are called at every moment to live out that request.

II. Psalms of Holy Communion

Communion, sadly, is considered a churchy word, dry as paper-thin wafers and spoken with the accompaniment of organ music rather than songs of honeymoon nightingales. Moreover, *communion*, when prefaced by *holy*, is elevated to the pious light of stained glass windows instead of being soaked in the ardent blue light of the full moon.

Yet, beneath these "spiritual" overlays, especially for those of the Christian tradition, communion implies a complete oneness with the Beloved. Communion is an opportunity to enter the zero gravity at the heart of the Gospel, the point of the fullness of no-self.

The following psalms are prayers that can be said before going to Holy Communion or as thanksgiving reflections afterwards. They are also daily prayers for those who aspire to live in communion with the Holy One.

79

Psalm of the Wide Open Gates
➽➻

Open wide every one of my portals, Beloved God,
   my eyes, ears, nose and mouth,
that I might be in full communion
   with all that I am.

Open wide every pore of my skin,
   so I can be in complete communion
with you, All Holy One,

present in all and everywhere.

Open wide every cell of my body,
    all flesh, bone, fluid and tissue,
so you, my Beloved Holy One, can be
    at home in all of me.

 Reflection: *Many of our devotional prayers invite God to live in our hearts and minds. Yet, those who think of God dwelling only in their hearts or minds unfortunately live below the poverty line! Only stingy lovers restrict how much of themselves is available to their lover.*

    "Off-Limits" and "No Trespassing" are unconscious signs posted on most of our body. Yet can even one's private parts be private in communion with God? Living in zero gravity erases such signs and dissolves such boundaries.

    This psalm-prayer is intended for use before or after Holy Communion to help us realize Christ is closer to us than we are to ourselves.

80

Holy Communion of Delight:
A Psalm of the Mouth
※≫≪≪

My mouth is heaven's gateway
    for communion with you, Beloved Christ.
My tongue tingles with your taste
    in the flavor of bread and wine.
A doorway of delight is my mouth,
    savoring you in food and drink.

Awaken, all you napping taste buds,
    to the flavor of God
in every shared meal or lonely lunch,
    for is not all food and drink
consecrated by God's desire for communion?

My mouth is heaven's gateway
    when I trace a cross on my lips
in your holy name, my Beloved;
    may every kiss imprint your sacred name
on the lips and hearts of others.

 Reflection: *The liturgical tradition of tracing the sign of the cross upon our lips at the reading of the Gospel can and should be used on other occasions. Doing so before prayer signals a desire to make our lips into instruments of praise. What better ritual could accompany the prayer of grace or blessing before and after a meal. Before kissing a child, friend, lover or spouse good night or when they are departing, to make the sign of the cross on our lips can consecrate the common into a sacrament.*

81

The Communion Psalm of True Lovers
❧❧ ❧❧

I ache with pain whenever you ache, O Christ,
    and yearn to steal away some, if not all,
of your past and present suffering,
    for though I feel so far away,

I long to be one in body and soul with you.

As a husband lovingly longs to bear
    the birth pains of his wife;
as a mother lovingly kisses away
    a child's pain from an injured finger,
I, your lover, wish to bear your cross.

I believe that when my love is great enough,
    when it rises from the depths of passion,
physical boundaries of space and time vanish,
    causing clocks to spin wildly backwards,
so that in mere minutes two millenniums have passed.

I pray, Suffering Beloved, that my compassion
    may suck out of your bleeding palms
the piercing pain of those sharp spikes,
    and I willingly embrace embarrassment
to remove some of your naked body's shame.

Lord, I am not worthy to share your pain,
    yet say but the word
and I will be united in full communion
    with you, my Suffering Savior.

 Reflection: *To believe the message of the First Letter of Peter might be considered grounds for insanity or heresy. In that epistle is the good news that we can rejoice to the degree we share in the sufferings of Christ (1 Peter 4: 13). Yet such a statement is not madness or heresy to lovers who suffer when they are unable to share in the pain of those they love. Accepting Peter's radical invitation to compassion is to fully embrace the zero gravity of Christ's passion, and to live fully.*

Only associates and friends flee from the cross of a beloved. Real lovers raise up ladders and nail themselves next to their beloved.

82

The Ladder Psalm of Lovers
꠸꠸꠸

As a lover might climb into the sickbed
   to be one with a dying beloved;
as, once, devoted ones climbed eagerly
   onto the funeral bonfire of a spouse,
so do I wish to climb love's ladder, O Christ,
   to a holy communion upon your cross.

I long with love's fierce blowtorch
   to weld my little pains and aches
to the cosmic wounds of your bruised body
   hanging tortured on death's tree.
I desire to know the ecstasy of communion
   through, in and with you.

When I try to escape from my suffering, Beloved,
   show me the ladder of love
by which I can climb into your embrace,
   so that you and I can be partners in pain,
co-redeemers, companion chain-breakers
   of all held prisoner by demon pain.

Whenever I doubt the communion of suffering,
   remind me, O Lord of Good Fridays and Easters,
that to share in your suffering and death
   is also to share in your resurrection.

Reflection: *St. Paul writes in Philippians (3: 8-10) what seems like heresy: "For his sake I accept the loss of all things . . . as so much rubbish . . . to know him . . . and share in his sufferings by being conformed to his death." He also tells us, "I have been crucified*

with Christ," and goes on to boast that Christ lives in him (Galatians 2: 19-20).

In some form or another suffering visits all of us daily. Each visitation is an invitation and a challenge to use the ladder of love and be joined with Christ on his cross, to enter the zero gravity of loving redemption. In order to transform suffering into redemption we must not hoard our pain and suffering, but, rather, we must give it away like Jesus did when he said, "This is my blood, the blood of the covenant, to be poured out on behalf of many" (Mark 14: 24).

83

Beware of the Dogs Psalm
⇒≫⋘⇐

Beware of the watchdogs of religion,
 how viciously they bark and bite.
Dobermans of dogma, thirsty for blood,
 Bible defenders, guard dogs of the literal.
Beware of the growling, heresy-hunting dogs
 prowling orthodoxy's rigid chain-link fences.

Beware of the dogged bird dogs,
 whose prey is the Spirit Dove in free flight.
Chained by fears, they are repelled
 by the freedom and liberty of love.
Beware, for they relentlessly sniff out the new,
 the Spirit's scent of novelty.

Beware of the snarling dogs of war,
 with the blood of God's wrath
 dripping from the corners of their fanged mouths,

from countless crusades,
bloodbaths and heretics aflame.
Beware of those who ravaged and shredded
with their sharp teeth
the apostles and prophets of old.
As Jesus said, rejoice, but also beware.

 Reflection: *Being in holy communion with Christ means being one with Jesus of Galilee in all that assailed him. The disciple of today meets far different difficulties than did disciples who lived in the diverse culture of two thousand years ago, yet in many ways the challenges are the same.*

"Beware of the dogs," warns St. Paul writing in Philippians (3: 2), "Beware of the evil-workers." Paul is not speaking of nonbelievers, but of fellow followers of the Risen Jesus who were fiercely opposed to the freedom of the Good News. Not only were they eager to keep the old laws and regulations, but they viciously attacked those who maintained the newness of the New Way.

"Beware of the Dogs" is a sign that could hang on any church door.

84

Psalm to a Common God
➔➤➤ ⟨⟨⟨⟨

My Friend and Lover, I speak to you
confident and assured.
For you are no high and mighty potentate
adorned with grand and lofty titles,

who demands abject adoration
>   or else heads will roll.

You are no majestic earthly ruler
>   that I need to address with deferential names.
Rather, you are my father, mother, friend and lover,
>   and I am your child and beloved.
So what need do I have of elaborate court ritual?

I can't scrape and crawl before you
>   when we're so intimate
>   and do everything together.
So I kiss your lips and not your shoes;
>   I hug not the ground, but you.

 Reflection: *When asked how to pray, Jesus gave his disciples a prayer that addressed God with a familiar name — a family name of father — a familiarity that must have shocked many. On numerous occasions in his own prayer, he likewise used this unregal household title. Of course, the proper etiquette of prayer would require addressing God with titles of greatness and grandeur, as once was required for the emperors of old.*

Such strict etiquette would further require never arguing with the Almighty, never objecting or disagreeing, and never speaking without finding some awesomely beautiful and majestic expression of praise. Naturally, it would also forbid dancing or making jokes with God Almighty.

This psalm should be accompanied by the one that follows, the Song of Awe, which complements and completes it. Together, these twin psalms can introduce us to the zero gravity that makes up the inner space of prayer.

85

The Song of Awe
⇒»«⇐

From that vast ocean that is you, O God,
   my heart can only sip a drop
without bloating to the point of explosion.

From that blazing sun that is you,
   my flesh can only endure a ray
without being charred into cinders.

From all the countless images that are you,
   my poor eyes can focus only on one or two
without being blinded by beauty.

Of all the names that speak of you
   my mind can grasp only a few
without being driven shell-shock mad.

Blessed are you, for you give yourself to me,
   in tiny droplets of the sea
rather than the vastness of the ocean.

Blessed are you, for you give yourself to me
   in a single yellow sun ray
and not in the nuclear furnace of the sun.

Blessed are you, for my eye and mind can encircle
   only so much glorious wonder.
Gracious are you to lovingly come to me
   in doses of holiness I can embrace.
More wholly other and awesome are you
   than anything I can know, feel, sense or see.
You are my Source and Beloved Destination.

Reflection: *This psalm of communion concludes this chapter and is a companion to the previous psalm and the other intimate prayers addressed to God. It flows from the vision of the prophet Isaiah when he had come to the temple in Jerusalem where God, the All Holy One, visited him in blinding, billowing clouds of glory heavy with frankincense, introduced by shattering thunderclaps and escorted by swarms of fierce six-winged angels proclaiming, "Holy, holy, holy." It's a vision that reminds us of God's awesomeness and transcendence as we pray.*

In contrast, the casualness with which holy things are handled, and the practice of addressing the Unspeakable Holy One and the Holy Son on a first-name basis reveal our belief in an all-too-common God, perhaps more appropriately spelled with a small "g."

The best lovers of God are those who pray with split-personalities, half intimately passionate lover and half awe-paralyzed adorer. In the zero gravity of true worship we constantly bounce between these completely opposite poles, sometimes within the same prayer.

Chapter 5
Psalms of the Gospel Age

I. Parable Psalms

 Jesus, with the Holy Spirit laced tightly to his tongue, revealed the joy-filled upside-down world of the kingdom of God on planet Earth. Earth was flipped upside down, causing the Star of Bethlehem to replace the magnetic North Star as the primary point of orientation. Magnetic fields were reversed for those who awakened to God's presence, and Earth was never to be the same again. To those who asked Jesus, "What is the reign of God like?" he answered by telling parables that were open to various explanations. Jesus' parable stories and parable lifestyle were a walking classroom on how to live in the holy zero gravity created by God's reign.

These story-parables as well as the parable-deeds performed by Jesus are constantly in need of being freed from the deadweight gravity of pulpits. When parables are earthbound by R-G, *religious gravity*, they fail to be windows into the wonderland of an Earth full of God. The teacher of Galilee's parables need once again to float in the zero gravity of the upside downdom, the kingdom of God in which Jesus continually lived and to which he invited his followers to take up their residence.

The following Gospel psalms have been sprinkled with the salt of the Spirit to make Jesus' parables and the Gospel's wisdom into zesty, chili-hot "wakeruppers." If, however, you prefer your religion on the bland side, easy to digest and guaranteed not to give you heartburn, you may want to be selective in praying from this chapter.

A Word of Caution: Praying these parable psalms may be harmful to your present religious gravity field.

86

The Good Samaritan Psalm
⋙⋘

In a muddy ditch, wounded and in pain,
   I prayed for help to you, my God.
A pastor ordained to be a helping hand,
   lost in his prayer, quickly passed by.
A lay minister came by, looking the other way,
   in a hurry, not wanting to be delayed.
In a muddy ditch I lay, wounded and in pain,
   and I prayed, "O God, come to my help."

A Samaritan stopped, smiled and stooped,
   and was your answer to my prayer.
A gay Samaritan, whose touch I shunned,
   was your angel in my great need.
I shuddered in shame as he anointed my wounds,
   lifted me in his arms and took me away.
I looked away, avoiding the innkeeper's eyes
   as he paid for my room and board, saying,
"I'll be back to see you in a few days."

You sent no seraph angel but a Samaritan;
   your answer, O God, was a mystery to me.
He was not one with whom I've ever shared a pew,
   or one with whom I'd ever share a meal.
Your answer came through one whom you'd condemned,

at least "they" said you had.
Help me, O Mysterious God,
    to understand the riddles you've hidden
inside your answers to my prayers.

 Reflection: *The parable of the Good Samaritan (Luke 10: 29-37) is not simply a good deed morality tale. It is a parable, an intertwined truth intended to be untangled. God's help in the parable comes to the robbed and wounded man from the least expected and least desirable source, a Samaritan, one despised by the Jews.*

Regardless of your sexual orientation, when next you are in great need and pray for God to come to your aid, be prepared for a Samaritan surprise. What would be the least expected source of assistance for you? Would you be shocked if God sent help through a gay, an ex-con, a person of another race or social class? Would you temporarily lose your grounded gravity if your rescuer were of a different religious or political persuasion — perhaps a drug dealer or a person with AIDS? Blessed are those who are shockproof disciples, for they shall never lose their true balance.

87

The Pharisee's Psalm
❧❧

O God, come to my assistance;
    O God, come to my help.
Faithfully I worship you every Sunday
    and return home feeling at peace.
I find it so hard to honestly pray,

"O God, pardon me, a sinner."

Daily, with devotion, I read from my Bible,
    finding righteousness in your words.
Every month I pray with my prayer group,
    finding joy and consolation there.
I enjoy a good standing in my church community
    and donate money to good causes.
So I find it hard to honestly pray,
    "I'm a sinner, O God, forgive me."

O God, come to my assistance;
    make haste to help me, I plead.
I even volunteer at a soup kitchen
    and feel good by feeding the poor.
I picket and boycott for your causes,
    secure in knowing I'm doing your good work.
So I find it hard to honestly pray,
    "O God, have mercy on me, a sinner."

O God, come quickly to my assistance;
    O God, make haste to help me.
With great dread I fear that I'm a Pharisee,
    while you are known to hear sinners' prayers.
O God, help me to be a good and holy person,
    who's also a wretch of a sinner.
Help me, O God, who hears the prayers
    of sorry sinful Pharisees.

Reflection: *Jesus' parable of the Pharisee and the publican about the self-righteous and sinners (Luke 18: 9-14) is just as relevant today as when it was told. Many Christians mouth prayers in which they call themselves sinners, yet they are more what theologian Robert Funk calls "honorary sinners." Jesus embraced as his friends the untouchables of his society, those who lived in the zero gravity of not having a self-righteous ground to stand on. He welcomed* honest sinners and challenged dishonest sinless saints to throw the first stone.

Honorary sinners are rarely scourged by sorrow. Rather than being exposed to the third degree, they are usually awarded an honorary degree. As honorary sinners we rigidly remain Pharisees when we have baptized our vices into virtues. We even let the good we do obscure our awareness of those baptized vices. Who can be grief-stricken about a sin dressed up as a pious virtue?

What is a baptized vice? It's making the letter of the law more important than the Spirit of the law, and making pious appearance more praiseworthy than love. Condemning the actions of others as evil and sinful — elevating it to a religious duty — baptizes the vice of judging others, so strongly forbidden by the Master. Subtly hidden within our religious principles can be a desire to make ourselves look better by putting others down. So include in your religious practice a regular search of your virtues to see if hidden in them are vices wearing fake halos. See how many of your principles you use as hammers, tools that can build the kingdom but may also be used to inflict injury. Then, even in the midst of your good deeds, you can pray the prayer of a genuinely sinful Pharisee.

88

The Sundowners' Psalm
❧»》《《❧

O Sunset Paymaster, the day is almost over;
    the sun is slowly sinking in the west.
Yet they come to work, only for an hour,
    while our sweaty backs are sore after a long hard day.
At the paymaster's table these unsweaty Sundowners
    who leisurely join us at the last hour

—who were last but now are first —
    are getting a full day's pay?

Not fair are your ways, O God, not fair,
    and you call yourself the God of Justice!
I've labored, done all you've asked — and more;
    I've kept the faith in times good and bad.
How can I swallow that the reward for all I've done
    is the same as the Johnnys-and-Janeys-come-lately?

We others have been your Johnnys-and-Janeys-on-the-spot
    when the church has needed repairs or dinners served.
I've signed my John Hancock to every church pledge,
    dug deep in my pocket for every foreign mission.
I've kept your hard commandments; I've paid my dues —
    surely, O God, my reward should be greater than theirs!

These sundowners, who come only for supper and a bed,
    are those unwilling to sweat and labor for you.
They're tramps, only after a free lunch at your table;
    your gift of salvation at sunset just isn't just!
Be reasonable, O God, be just,
    make your reward fit the deeds
as the punishment fits the crime.

Now that I've said my piece, O God, I pray,
    forgive my anger
and help me understand that your parable ways
    are not our ways.

Reflection: In Australia, "Sundowner" is the term for a tramp. In former times it referred to a person who went from ranch to ranch, arriving just at sundown, too late to have to do much work, but in time for the evening meal. The parable of Jesus in Matthew (20: 1-16) is a theological tale of God's justice and love toward the workers in the vineyard. Jesus presents a just God, who pays his

workers what he promised. Then the upside downdom of the kingdom reveals a wildly and wondrously free God, able to be as shockingly generous as was the father in the parable of the prodigal. As we saw in the chapter on devotional prayers, such a love creates its own zero gravity field which supersedes the normal gravity field.

Jesus concludes the tale with a paradox that causes some believers to lose their former well-grounded gravity of faith: The sundowners will be the sunrisers, and the sunrisers will be the sundowners — the first will be the last, and the last will be first. This psalm can be an occasion to check your Who's Who directory of good and bad people and then turn that list upside down. It can help you realize that you may share your eternal reward on equal footing with last-minute emigrants to the kingdom who had been child molesters, criminals executed by capital punishment and drug dealers.

89

The Lost Sheep Psalm
⇒≫ ≪⇐

O God, bend low and hear my prayer;
    O God, be not deaf to my plea.
I am your lost sheep, who seeks to be found
    and has not even left the ninety-nine.
They, the flock, press in upon and around me,
    bleating loudly their prayers to you.
I cannot breathe, suffocated by your sheep;
    O Good Shepherd, come and find me.

I'm lost in the flock, yearning to be found by you;

my Beloved Shepherd, O hear my cry.
I'm trampled underfoot as they herd their way
     to greener pastures and safer paths.
I'm blinded by the dust of their retreating feet,
     as they scurry away from risky justice.
I'm deaf from the rattle of their tin-can prayers,
     vacant, empty of any passion and love.

O Jesus, the Risen One, my Good Shepherd,
     I seek the warm embrace of your love.
For chilly as winter is the flock's legal love,
     as they bleat out in refrain,
     "Sorry, but the law says . . . ."
They're no pilgrim flock, but a marching army,
     following a drummer whose beat I cannot hear.
Yet I wonder, is it I who am lost among the ninety-nine
     and so seek to be found by you,
or is it you, the Good Shepherd, who must be found?

Which causes greater joy in heaven and on earth,
     the finding of one lost sinner sheep
or the finding of you, my beloved lost Good Shepherd?

 Reflection: *The Trappist monk Thomas Merton said he felt himself to be an alien as he prayed and lived in his monastery. To be an alien on foreign soil in a strange land is bad enough. But it's even more painful to feel alienated in your own home or church — a most radical kind of inner zero gravity.*

Jesus' parable of the Good Shepherd, who left the ninety-nine to find the one lost sheep (Luke 15: 3-7) can be a source of hope for those who feel like aliens yet have never left home. This parable is also a paradoxical invitation for us to be found in the process of leaving home in search of the shepherd.

90

The Gambler's Psalm
⇒》《⇐

Lord of the loaded dice,
    God of gamblers and card sharks,
  hear this poor fainthearted plea.
Give me a lover's heart,
    willing to gamble all,
    everything I own, on thee.

Give me not a banker's or accountant's heart,
    lest I calculate the cost
    of loving you.
Calculators carefully measure
    potential risk and profit;
    gamblers go on a spree, play a hunch.
O God of crazy men and women,
    give to me, I plead,
    the heart of a gambler and a lover.

For, my Beloved,
    I've seen your treasure,
    playfully hidden in a "field" for me to find.
My eyes have seen it, more than once;
    my lips have savored its wet delight;
    my fingers have caressed it many times.
My ears have heard its exotic music,
    but I've feared to gamble everything,
    all I hold dear, in order to possess it.

Not being an impulsive gambler,
    I'm making layaway deposits on the field.
Can you, O God who's worth the risk,
    love me, a cautious lover?

Reflection: *Jesus said that entering the reign of God is like the happy-ending parable of the person who discovered a buried treasure in a field (Matthew 13: 44). He quickly reburied the precious treasure and raced home. With joy he sold all he owned and bought the field. This, Jesus said, is what it means to find the kingdom of God.*

In the treasure hunt of life, we can see the tip of treasures hidden in what is seen, tasted, touched and heard. Yet most of us don't expect to find a holy treasure in these earthy sights, sounds and tastes. Perhaps if we dig more deeply into these common gifts of life, we might unearth the priceless treasure of the reign of God.

In a cloud of incense, we can also stumble over the tip of the treasure: a Godly iceberg, so to speak, in the "fields" of our prayer times or Sunday worship. With ninety percent of the treasure hidden from view, most of us simply genuflect and go about our business.

Yet perhaps the real reason we hurry on is that we lack a gambler's heart. We stay on the surface of life, with it's safe and modest rewards. Yet if we took a risk and went deeper, we might discover something eminently worth the gamble. The next time you taste an earthy delight or genuflect at a Godly iceberg, pause on one knee and scratch beneath the surface to see if you can find the treasure.

When you have discovered the treasure and see it in all its beauty and splendor, then pray the Gambler's Psalm or even this short prayer:

> *O God, help me learn the Gambler's Golden Rule:*
> *To win everything, I must gamble everything,*
> *everything I have.*

91

Let Those with Noses Smell:
The Searching for God Psalm
❧≫≪❧

The fragrance I recognize
is not frankincense
but the roselike aroma
of your delicate beauty, O Beloved.
Unable to resist, I push my nose
as deeply as I can into you.

As clergy cautiously tiptoe
round your guarded sanctuary gate,
I sniff the clouds of incense
and stretch my nose searchingly,
seeking for your scent in church.

I also breathe in deeply the holy odor
of your scent mixed within the sweat
from the hard work of a job well done,
the odor rising from any long labor of love —
reaching my nose as the wet scent of your lovemaking.

I even smell your sacred presence
in the bedpan fragrance of nursing homes,
in hospital wards and hospice death houses,
where your hidden holy work of care
stinks to the high heavens.

Creator God, give me a dog's nose
a million times keener
at scents and smells than mine,
so that, like a bloodhound,
wherever I go, I can track you down.

Reflection: *Jesus played with riddles of eyes and ears: "Let those with eyes see, and those with ears hear" (see Mark 4: 9-10). He was not speaking to those who were literally blind or deaf, yet the majority of his audience saw and heard nothing different from what they expected to see and hear.*

Invisible to the eye and inaudible to the ear is a source of knowledge provided by the nose. The average person can detect more than ten thousand different odors. Moreover, the human brain doesn't have space to store and keep track of all the possible combinations of smells, which may be as many as ten thousand. So the mind focuses on smells that have been most relevant in its evolution, like the pleasing odor of ripe fruit or the magnetic scent of a sexually receptive mate.

We are made in the divine image. Since God created such a wondrous body for us — including an exquisitely perceptive and sensitive nose — are we not able to detect the smell of God, the rare, exotic perfume of the Presence? Such an awareness can lead us to pray:

O God, may my nose get drunk today on your perfume.

92

The Light of the World Psalm
❧❧❧

O God, how lonely it is
   to be the light of the world,
to be your justice and love
      in a world devoid of them,
to be kindness and compassion

in a world of competition.
Yes, I find it lonely being luminous.

I feel like the sun, the blazing day-star
    which gloriously illuminates our world,
a sun-star so large you could place
    a million Earths inside of it,
as alone as a single comet in the vastness of empty space,
    laboring to be the light of the world.

If our giant orb of a sun
    were shrunk to the size of a basketball
and placed hanging over New York City,
    the closest sun-star to it
would be another glowing basketball
    suspended over Honolulu, Hawaii.

As all-alone as our solitary sun,
    at times, that's how I feel, Radiant God.
How hard to be the light of the world,
    to hold a glowing warmth in a world so cold.
So forgive me, Beloved, for being
    just a momentary shooting star
in the darkness of my world.

 Reflection: *Jesus often spoke in parable-pictures — as when he called his disciples to be salt and light (Matthew 5: 3-16). He said to us, "You are the light of the world." What an awesome challenge the Master gave to his disciples: to be like the sun. While looking up from Earth, the night sky seems crowded with stars; in reality, the space between these galactic suns is vast. The distance is so great that it must be measured in light-years rather than miles. Our sun-star's closest neighbor is Alpha Centauri, which is 4.3 light years away — and light travels at 670 million miles per hour!*

    Jesus must have felt as solitary as our sun in his struggle to enlighten his world. To be one with the Beloved Master includes

sharing the loneliness of being light. Even surrounded with a circle of friends and disciples, Jesus, Buddha and Mohammed all must have experienced the isolation of outer space as God set them ablaze with love in a sea of darkness.

Ninety-nine percent of disciples prefer to be moons that only reflect the light of their Star-Savior Suns. Rather than burning with love for God, their light only faintly mirrors the light of the stars they orbit. Jesus, however, did not say, "You are the moon of the world." So, each of us must choose today what we will be: a sun or a moon.

93

The Lamp Psalm
❖❖❖

My God, help me come out from under my bed,
    bringing my lamp out into the night.
In fear, I light my lamp and then
    put it and myself under my bed,
afraid that my deeds of light
    will dangerously glow in the dark.

Help me, O God, for fearfully I walk and work
    with my light under a bushel basket,
afraid that those who hate the light, night's secret police,
    will spy my light and snuff it out,
casting me into the darkness as well.

Help me to come out from under my bed,
    boldly holding up my light.
Help me cast aside my bushel basket
    and let my light truly shine,

as I thumb my nose at the dark's secret police.

You are a God who loves secret prayers
    and hidden acts of kindness.
Show to me your holy secret
    of how to expose my light to the world
in hidden deeds of light and love.

Reflection: *Seeming contradictions abound with the Master. First, he sternly orders us to make our good works secret and hidden (Matthew 6: 1-6), and then he tells us they should be brought out into the light (Mark 4: 21). The disciple is thrown into the zero gravity of needing to ponder and sort through such paradoxes in order to be creatively faithful to Jesus' words.*

How then are we to let our inner light shine, since we are called to pray under our bed and give alms wearing a bushel basket? The Master was aware that praise causes a dangerous wind to rise, so do nothing to earn yourself praise and recognition, lest that praise huff and puff out your light.

One translation of Philippians 4: 5 illuminates a way to safely let our light shine forth: "Let your unselfishness be known by all." Modern translations phrase it, "Your kindness should be known by all." Being kind at all times to all persons requires the zero gravity of being unselfish to a very high degree — so perhaps the two translations are the same.

This suggests that being kind to others can act as a safety windbreaker against the high winds that threaten our exposed light. For simply being kind is unobtrusive, hardly worthy of praise. No halos are handed out to kind people. In fact, being unselfish in all things, putting others and their needs first, isn't even viewed as a positive virtue in the psychology of self-esteem.

Play with this paradox. Not in grand gestures of giving away all you own to the poor or in glorious religious deeds of fasting or prayer, but simply by being unselfish will you shine like the sun, and so give glory to God.

94

The Corn Psalm

⇒≫≪⇐

Teach me, O God, to be like the peasant farmer
who sows his corn seeds in the soil
and knows not how or why they sprout,
    mysteriously growing tall while he sleeps.
Enlighten me, for hidden in the inner wisdom of corn seeds
    is the secret of spiritual growth.

Green sprouts spring out of the seed, O Divine Gardener,
    and strain upward through the soil.
Sun-stroked and rain-fed into growing tall,
    they bear bountiful ears full of golden grain
that ripening, hear your blessed harvest song.

A great mystery is all this to the faithful farmer,
    who at night does not need to go out
to pull up and tug at the tiny plant,
    or huff and puff all day long
to make his corn grow tall and strong.

O Divine Mystery, may I not wring my hands in anxiety,
    searching for some all-knowing guru
to guide my growth in prayerful grace,
    to assure my bearing a golden holy harvest.
Let me only plant my little self-seed
    in your rich soil, O God, and then simply let go.

Reflection: *Jesus gives excellent instructions for emigrating to the kingdom of God and for growing in personal holiness, which is only letting the fullness of God's reign grow within us (Mark 4: 26).*
The good news of the Gospel's zero gravity is that we need

not fret about methods and techniques, classes or conferences to attend, about what books to read or finding the right guru at whose feet we can sit. The work of God's kingdom mysteriously takes place within us even when we sleep.

Growing in holiness and into the reign of God, however, does not mean doing nothing. A good farmer doesn't take a vacation during growing season. Like a good farmer, we need to remove the weeds ever so cautiously, to till the crusted earth so it can breathe, to talk to our crops and when necessary to irrigate. Yet a loving farmer needs no university expert to guide him in how to grow his corn. He trusts in the ancient mystery of a good seed buried in good soil, in every seed's passionate desire to grow up into a plant.

As the Corn Psalm proclaims, we need a zero-gravity trust in the nature of all seeds; the secret of the kingdom of God and our spiritual growth says that we need to let go and not fret.

95

A Psalm of the Dangers of Reconciliation
➵➤➤⋘⋘

I've just been given absolution, O God,
    and I need to make this prayer to you.
All my sins have been wiped away,
    and my house heart is swept clean.
Cleansed of guilt and all evil,
    my old dark demon has been evicted.
Gone is my enticer into sin,
    yet the Master warns that there's a danger here.

"Go now in peace" is reconciliation's refrain,
    a farewell invitation to return home
to a freshly swept Easter abode of new life.

Yet "Go in peace, but also take care,"
   is what I need to hear,
for my evicted evil one,
   when tired of wandering homeless,
will gather up seven more evil demons
   to come home and live with me again.

Woe that this should be my fate
   in my forgiven state of grace,
that my newfound clean and ordered space
   should be worse than my old and sinful state.
Help me, Merciful God, to be on guard,
   yet even great guardedness is not enough.
To keep my heart-home free and clean,
   I must invite you, Beloved,
to be my permanent guest.

Reflection: Jesus gives a serious warning to those who have had an exorcism, who have been cleansed by confession or reconciliation. He advises us to guard well our doors, lest the demon who has been thrown out might return again but this time with seven more evil, fiendish friends (see Luke 11: 24-26).

Absolved of sin, before returning home renewed, we need to pray for help. We can ask ourselves prayer-questions like any wise host or hostess would ask, "Will my evicted evil house guest, upon returning, knock or ring my door bell — or will the fiend sneak in through the basement window? Will my old diabolic guest and seven evil friends come back disguised as angels? If so, how can I tell a real angel from a costumed white-winged demon?"

Does Jesus imply that the devil we know is better than the seven we don't? Is it, then, better to go back to our old ways than to try to maintain a clean heart? Yet all evil is a parasite, is insidious. This psalm and the next one, the Plower's Psalm, address some of these prayer-questions and suggest that the only sure answer is to set our hearts on the Beloved.

96

The Plower's Psalm

*orget what lies behind you
once you put your hand to the plow,
for you may plow a crooked furrow
or run your plow headlong into a rock.

I hear the wise advice of Jesus
to keep my vision only forward,
to look not at what lies to the right or left,
but only at what remains unplowed ahead.

So, Master, set down securely on my shoulders
your starch-collared yoke
to keep me from turning my head around
to look at where I've been.

"Let the dead bury the dead," I also say,
pushing on without regret over past deeds,
over previous decisions or old life-patterns,
focusing only on the goal of new life.

Direct me, Harvest Master, in your Way,
guiding my plow for what lies ahead,
to labor as a single-visioned plower
in the field where I hope to find your treasure.

Reflection: *St. Paul and Jesus spoke the same agrarian wisdom, that whatever success or failure may have filled your old field, forget it. In Philippians (3: 13), Paul said, "Forget what lies behind and strain forward." Jesus gave this advice to those eager to labor at plowing the field of the reign of God, "Once you put your hand to the plow, never look backwards" (Luke 9: 62).*

Both Jesus and Paul spoke like explorers of new lands whose vision was locked on what was yet to be discovered. The danger in looking backwards is that the gravity fields of our past worlds will hold us back and keep us from emigrating to the kingdom of God.

The zero-gravity message of the Gospel is: Don't let your vision or your direction in life boomerang, or you'll get stuck in the past, never making it to the new world of God's reign. Don't regret your previous decisions or look longingly back at what once was, or today you may plow a crooked furrow or, worse yet, miss the buried treasure.

97

Psalm of the Chemistry Lesson
➔⟫ ⟪←

O Holy Wisdom Teacher, instruct me,
	for I wish to be your eager student
in the cosmic chemistry class of conflicts
	and their secret creative power.

I've been a dunce in your class, I fear,
	failing to imaginatively experiment
with the full measure of conflicts
	that you've poured into my life.

I've failed to fill my life's test tube
	with my problems and challenges,
desiring to conduct my experiments
	with only the simpler substances,
like happiness, success, pleasure and the promise
	of a string of bright, sunny days.

Thus failing to test my trials and crosses

for hidden gifts of gratitude and wisdom,
I have failed to tap into a valuable resource
    containing great life-energy and creativity.
Help me today, Master Teacher,
    to be a better chemist in your art of love.

 Reflection: *To be a true disciple of the Master of Galilee is to accept an invitation to be a chemist in the laboratory of conflict experimentation. Certain chemical reactions move us to zero gravity, where* we discover that a downer in life can easily become an upper. This shift in gravity produces a reversal in the normal order of things, a shift to the social and spiritual values which Jesus incarnated.

This gravity makes daily life more adventuresome and fun than any loop-the-loop roller coaster. Jesus' call to chemistry is found in his invitation, "If you wish to be my disciple, take up your cross and follow me into the laboratory of love" (see Matthew 16: 24-25).

Conflicts, when mixed with equal parts of gratitude and love, become growth hormones capable of creating giants of the soul. Conflicts, when stirred vigorously with the pestle of the cross, become supercharged with nuclear electrons able to light up the world. The next time a cross is dropped into your lap, rather than putting on a sorrowful face, put on your white laboratory jacket.

98

Psalm for Healing the Tongue
→»·«←

eloved Master, touch my mouth
    with your freeing finger,

dripping in your healing saliva,
    so my poor tamed tongue
may miraculously be un-tongue-tied,
    liberated to speak boldly of you.

For I'm a lover with a dull tongue,
    unable to proclaim with passion,
ashamed of bedroom words of love,
    embarrassed to let my tongue
declare my true affection for you.

My tongue has been rendered tame
    by stiffly embalmed words.
Formed in childhood and in church,
    unable now to arouse me,
are my soulless words of prayer.

Jesus, son of David, heal my tongue,
    and my mouth will freely proclaim
my unbridled love for you.

 Reflection: *Jesus healed the blind and gave the gift of speech to those who were speechless (see Matthew 10: 27-33). His healing of the afflicted, however, is not restricted to the past. We are all invited to call upon the Risen Jesus to heal us.*

Tongue-tied lovers, like the one in this psalm, fill church pews to overflowing. Perhaps those of us so afflicted would blush when asked by the healing Master, "Would you like me to cure you and set your tongue on fire?"

This pre-prayer ritual of desire for healing could precede the praying of any psalm or prayer: Take your tongue between your thumb and index finger and close your eyes for a moment. Releasing your tongue and opening your eyes, exclaim, "Dance and leap, lame tongue, to the delight of your Maker."

II. Psalms of the Holy Spirit

When Jesus told his disciples that he must return to the Father, they were greatly distressed. They feared his impending departure would cause them to be cast from the enormous gravity of his physical presence into the zero gravity of loss. As their beloved Master, he was their grounding in the new world, the kingdom of God, to which they had emigrated in response to his invitation to follow him. As he spoke to them about his leaving, they must have felt the very ground beneath their feet shifting, beginning to slide away from under them.

Aware of their anxiety, Jesus promised them that he would not leave them as orphans, as aliens adrift without support, but would send them his Spirit, the Paraclete.

Christians faithfully credo their fundamental belief in a God who is a community of three: Father, Son and Spirit. Since the physical departure of Jesus, the predominant presence in the church has been the Spirit of the Holy. Yet in day-to-day living, disciples appear to focus more on the Father and the Son than on the third person. While periods of charismatic interest rise and fall like ocean waves, the absence of the Spirit is especially notable in the area of ongoing daily prayer. Christians usually pray *to* the Father and Son, even if *in* and *through* the Holy Spirit.

The Spirit of God, present in the First Testament, the Hebrew Scriptures, becomes more prominent in the Second Testament. The whole Acts of the Apostles is a diary of the power of the Spirit present in the early church. It portrays the action of the Spirit in the lives and world of the disciples and those whom they attracted to the zero gravity of the reign Jesus came to establish. That dynamic Holy Presence, however, is not limited to the age of the apostles. To live in Gospel time is to live in a Spirit-soaked zone in which this Holy Power is a daily and active agent.

As you pray the following psalm-prayers that are about or addressed to the Holy Spirit, be mindful of the promised Paraclete of Jesus as a new gravity field in your life.

99

Psalm of the Name of the Holy Spirit

To pray in the name of the Father
    is to begin and end a prayer
in the awesome presence of the Godhead.

To pray in the name of the Son
    is to use the name of names
that makes all prayer instantly heard.

To pray in the name of the Holy Spirit
    is to invoke the power to create,
to inspire, inflame and consecrate all
    upon whom that name is spoken.

So with faith in the promised gift of Jesus, I pray:
    In the name of the Creative Spirit,
I dedicate each work, ever eager for newness.
    In the name of the Holy Spirit,
I begin and end every holy work and prayer.
    In the name of the Life Spirit,
I struggle to raise dead things to life.
    In the name of Heaven's Wind,
I set sail for all unknown destinations.
    In the name of Heaven's Fire,
I torch awake sleeping, drugged hearts.
    In the name of God's Holy Breath,
I enkindle into flame dying embers of hope.

In the name of God's Holy Finger,
I follow divine direction to find the Way.

In the name of the ancient Prophets' Spirit,
may I boldly proclaim the reign of God today,
that realm promised of old by the Father and the Son
that exists beneath my feet and at my fingertips.
May I smash open prison-door locks
so that those incarcerated as I am,
prisoners confined in defeat and depression's dungeon,
can come forth into the glorious freedom
of a new day birthed by the Spirit of God.

Amen. So be it today, tomorrow,
and all tomorrows without end.

 Reflection: *Whatever task is before you, begin it in the name of the Holy Power so the stream of the Spirit of God's power can cascade upon you like a waterfall and flow through all your efforts.*

When you are tired, let the Spirit refresh your sagging spirit and energize your stagnant soul as you slowly savor one of the countless names of the Holy Spirit. When coming to the Third Person in the Sign of the Cross, consider using one of the Spirit's variety of names as the situation requires.

100

Psalm of the Holy Power
⋙⋘

I n the name of the Father
and of the Son and of the Holy Power.

In the name of the Holy Power, may I be kind
    when I'm needled toward the edge of rudeness.
In the name of the Holy Power, may I be patient
    when I'm at the end of my rope.
In the name of the Power to be nonjudgmental,
    may I have the discipline to not be judge and jury.
In the name of the Power to pardon, may I forgive
    when I've grown tired of practicing forgiveness.

In the name of the Power of Confirmation,
    may I affirm others as I wish to be affirmed.
In the name of the Power to be brave, may I be strong
    when I am fearful and feeling cowardly.
In the name of the Power of the prophets,
    may I not fear to speak out or be out of line.
In the name of the Holy Power of Godliness,
    may I be Godlike when I wish to be only human.

In the name of the Holy Power of Love,
    may I love greatly when God becomes routine,
when my prayer life seems merely an obligation,
    and religion only a blessed business with a bottom line.

Reflection: *Spirit, like the older form, Ghost, is a vapor word. Other than when it is combined with team, it seldom carries a zestful punch. Yet the Spirit of God is the animating force of life, the bestower of the essential gifts, which are presents of power.*

Until Jesus was baptized and filled with the Holy Spirit's gifts, he apparently did nothing worthy of recording in the pages of the four Gospels. Once empowered by God's Holy Power, however, all heaven seemed to break loose. By our baptism into Christ, that same Holy Power has been bestowed on us. What wonders might happen in our lives and our world if we took that gift of power seriously?

101

Psalm of the Brooding Spirit
-»»-«««-

ome, Spirit of the Holy, brood over me,
   huddling henlike as you once did
over the dark, swirling waters of chaos
   on Creation Eve.

Your scream shattered the silence
   as God's love cracked open the cosmic egg,
spilling out spiral galaxies and stars,
   planets and moons, oceans and land.

Brood over me, Spirit of Creation,
   with your searing, scarlet wings aflame.
Umbrella me in the hothouse steam of love,
   so my hard shell will shatter open.

Then, spill forth from the very center of me
   God's wildest dreams and fantasies,
heaven's highest hopes for my day and times,
   as you again recreate this old, weary world.

Reflection: *This psalm of the Spirit-Agent of Creation is a song-prayer which can be used any morning or as a pre-work psalm for those who are laborers of the new covenant, that unique zero-gravity order of life which calls for perpetual newness.*

Brooding, as a hen does while hatching an egg, takes time. So allow appropriate incubating space and time for the warmth of the brooding God to influence you in a time of seeming chaos. Also consider calling for a "silent prayer time of brooding" at meetings when a stalemate locks shut the floodgates of creative resolution.

102

Bury the Dead Psalm:
A Prayer of the Holy Spirit's Shovel
❖

weet Anointing from above,
ooze your oil of mercy onto me
so, Tobit-like, I too can bury the dead.

Old Tobit risked death to bury the dead
as God's Spirit shoveled him out of bed,
cultivating in him the courage and reverence
to perform his noble work.

Anoint me with the oil of compassion
as I tend to the dead before they die.
Give me words to praise all the good they've done
and the influence they've had on others,
to affirm the value and meaning of their lives
and to sing of their sacrifices made out of love.

Holy Anointer, appoint me to your work
of investing with dignity, grace and pride
those who are nearer to death than I,
to fill the pockets of their hearts
with the gold of gratitude,
so they may go to their graves with honor,
knowing the satisfaction of a bountiful harvest.

Reflection: *One of the holy works of the Holy Spirit is burying the dead. This was considered an important work of mercy to be shared by everyone in former days before the task of burial became a business in our society. St. Tobit of the First Testament is the patron saint of those who go apart from their daily work, even being*

dragged away from their sleep, to give proper burial to the dead.

Today's science often merely prolongs life, so that the aged become the living dead. To bury the dead with dignity is a work that begins before death. The Spirit is eager to help us praise the aged with floral wreathes of congratulations for their efforts to bring their youthful dreams to bloom. The Spirit empowers us to erect monuments in their presence to how their life victories have overshadowed their defeats, to attest to the value of their lives.

Attending a wake or funeral service is an expression of this corporal work of mercy. This psalm suggests how to practice this work of the Spirit in another way. It shows how we can eulogize people before they die, allowing them, so to speak, to be awake at their own wake.

103

Ashes to Ashes: A Psalm of the Holy Spirit
≈≫≪≈

Holy Fire of God,
 descend as once you did in times of old,
furnace full of searing flames
 engulfing ancient Mount Sinai
in the fullness of God's presence.

Fire Storm of the Holy,
 wind-sweep your wall of flame over me
in a raging Pentecostal love,
 and burn me to ashes, again.

Ages before ages past, my flesh was once
 the glowing ashes of a dead sun
drifting to Earth as star-flakes
 to become again the stuff of life.

No mere dark clay or Earth-dirt am I,
for star-studded space was my womb.
Ashes to ashes, star dust to star dust,
so bury me now in the passion of God's Furnace
so I can rise, phoenix-like,
to a new way of living and loving.

 Reflection: *The story of Earth's creation is about cremation. God created Adam not from the clay of the Earth but from the ashes of cremated stars. This is a powerful image of life coming out of death, of the funeral pyre becoming a birthing bed. It leads us to ask if the natural way to deal with death may not be holy fire instead of decay. Rather than a funeral feast for worms, perhaps a Viking hero's bonfire burial is a more fitting end.*

Along with the sun, fire was once worshipped as divine — as a god or a gift from the gods. In our age of electric fires and lights, the flames of fire might be newly reverenced as holy. It is a rich symbol of our star-dust origins as well as an image of our funeral-pyre rebirth in the flames of God's passionate love.

104

Psalm of The Holy Engine
⋙⋘

O Spirit of God, who once drove Jesus
into the desert to pray,
propel me now into prayer and praise.

O Energy of God, electrify my sluggish heart

to whirl out in wonder
passionate prayers of God's love.

O Holy Spirit, spin me wildly and freely,
       dancing in your holy whirlwind,
as once you revolved within and around Jesus.

O Enthusiasm of the Prophets, spark me now
       into flames of zeal to speak for God
in your ever daring and audacious ways.

O Expeller of Demons, be my holy broom
       to sweep out the evil spirits
that make my soul and God's good world unclean.

O Generator of Creation, stir up deep within me
       heaven's fiery creativity
in fixing meals, in making love, in all life.

 Reflection: *For some, coffee is the energizing agent to start them humming at the beginning of a new day; for others, it is a breakfast of champions. Early morning, midday or during low-energy afternoons — regardless of the time — consider using the Spirit of God as your energy booster.*

The Spirit was the hidden engine inside Jesus that propelled him into the desert to be alone with God. The Spirit moved Jesus to attend dinners where the guests were outcasts and God's fallen-aways. The Spirit spurred him to stand up boldly before pious bigots and powerful procurators of Rome.

Wrapped tightly as a prisoner in perfumed burial shrouds, Jesus was powerless in death. Then the same Spirit of Life who conceived Jesus in the womb rendezvoused to do the same in the womb of the tomb. The Spirit bent low and breathed new vitality into the lifeless Jesus, catapulting him out of the grave in an Easter ascension that was forever beyond the grasp of death. It was the greatest prison break in all history, and it's an escape that's also been promised to you and me.

Frequently call upon the Great Liberator from all prisons. Daily be with this Holy Source of Power so that your most important and very last request of the Spirit will be fulfilled.

105

Pentecostal Psalm of No-Tongues
━━➤➤ ⳦⳦━━

Blowtorch Spirit-Giver of Gifts,
    who descended as flaming tongues
on the disciples knotted together in prayer,
    come now aflame in me.
Twist my tongue into a fiery knot,
    so tight as to be speechless.

Give me no foreign mystical tongue
    to amaze and astonish all,
but the tongue of a wonder-rooted tree,
    whose bark sings with silvery gray silence,
or the mute tongue of an awestruck rock,
    whose poetry is forever petrified.

God's Spirit of Holy Construction,
    who lovingly builds up the Church,
gently clamp my teeth together
    lest my tongue tear Christ's Body to pieces.
Guide me to listen, instead of speak,
    so I can understand rather than stand over.
By so silencing my talking ego,
    may I become speechless, a Spirit-tongued lover,
who reverences and nourishes awesome life.

Reflection: *To reduce the size of the self, shutting our mouth is far better than harsh penances and ascetical self-denial. Because the tongue is a tool of self-promotion, consider using that tool less to build up yourself and more to build up the Body of Christ. The Spirit's gift of being tongueless is a mute tool toward silent communion with others, creation and God.*

Listen instead of speaking when others complain. Listen instead of joining in when others are being condemned. As St. Paul said in Galatians: "If you go on biting and tearing one another to pieces, take care; you will end up in mutual destruction!" (Galatians 5: 15). Listen instead of speaking when others are starving for the spotlight, and you will feed the hungry. Listen totally to those who thirst not for advice but only for someone to listen, and you will give them the water of life. Listen instead of speaking, and you will cultivate the capacity to be struck with awe at the wonder of life.

Many are those who are incarcerated in the cage of the ego. To be tongue-tied by the Spirit, however, is not to be a prisoner but to be free as a bird.

Chapter 6

Psalms of Suffering, Lamentation and Repentance

 Suffering, mourning and sinfulness remove our normal gravity, the life supports and structures that keep us grounded in our daily lives. This chapter provides prayers for these temporary states of zero gravity in which our usual stability is swept away.

Those who suffer from various afflictions and pains for long periods of time could be said to exist in the zero gravity of suffering, which so upsets the regular routines and rhythms of life. Long-term sickness deports us to a totally foreign world, as does the death of a loved one.

The reality of pain and suffering is the great test of our faith in a loving God. Jesus, in the prayer he gave us, the Lord's Prayer, directs us to ask that we not be led into temptation, and suffering may be the greatest of temptations. In the Garden of Gethsemani his agony gave rise to the ancient question "Why?" He asked that agonized question drenched in sweat and blood and in dread at his approaching trial of great pain and death.

Faith in a loving, gentle, all-good God is threatened by seemingly senseless pain. Yet in the mortal agony of Jesus of Galilee upon his ugly cross can be found a way to decode death and find meaning in our suffering.

The second section of this chapter contains psalms of lamentation. These are prayers of anguish which give voice to our deepest groans and grieving. Lamentations are not out of place for those who believe in the victory of life after death. They are simply natural responses to the loss of what and whom we greatly love.

The third section deals with regret, confession and reconciliation. One psalm suggests how our conscience itself can be a source of suffering and sorrow when we fail to do good. Other psalm-prayers show how all suffering causes a shift in our gravity field. A small word spoken to us in haste or anger can cause us to be knocked off our feet. We may be thrown off balance by our anger toward the one responsible for stealing our gravity and casting us adrift in a sea of pain. Guilt also disorients us, and this section suggests that in its wake we need to seek reconciliation as a way to regain our equilibrium and return to a normal, healthy life.

I. Psalms of Suffering

This section contains psalm-prayers that address the disorientation created by suffering. Pain comes to us in many flavors: the pain of a minor illness or a lethal sickness, the pain of a headache or a heartache. However it appears, pain steals away the calm and ease of the normal gravity of everyday life and throws us into the disorientation of zero gravity.

106

Psalm of Living in the All
➺⟫⟪⟫

Help me, Compassionate God,
> to find relief in my suffering.
You who are within all things,
> help me to live outside myself.
Help me live in the all in which you exist,
> to find a new identity
which is greater than myself.

Expand my frontiers wider than my skin
> to encompass an eagle's far-reaching flight.
Enlarge me to the height of a Douglas fir,
> to a Spirit-bird's-eye perspective.
Broaden my boundaries beyond the orbits
> of Jupiter and Mars
to embrace the vastness of the universe.

Stretch me so as to live in the all,
　　　　as I struggle to escape the prison
of my terrible pain and suffering
　　　　that restricts me to my personal needs.
O God of Boundless Love, expand my horizons
　　　　to that place of no horizons
so that I can live in you.

O God, help me escape my prison of pain.

 Reflection: *Herman Melville, author of Moby Dick, wrote a letter to his author-friend Nathaniel Hawthorne, in which he quoted the lines of Johann Goethe, "Live in the all." Melville, however, suggested that when we're held prisoner by a toothache Goethe's advice is nonsense!*

It is precisely in moments of suffering or grief at the death of someone or something we love that our heart frontiers are constricted. Whenever we must endure great pain, we are challenged to find and emigrate to a new and better place.

Pain can be embraced as a natural part of life or suffered as a curse from God. Of course, every form of medical and psychological healing should be employed to avoid or relieve pain. The suffering that cannot be alleviated, however, must be explored as a departure point — not so much to escape but to find inside the pain a new place of meaning and purpose.

Pain is the prison warden that keeps us locked in the world of suffering. "To live in the all" is a freedom tunnel. Like all escape tunnels, it requires the hard work of digging oneself out of captivity. Even if you cannot extend yourself as far as the rings of Jupiter, try to emigrate to a larger realm than your present pain-shrunk world.

107

The Psalm of Shared Pain
⇒》《⇐

In pain shared, my pain is lessened;
 this wisdom is hidden in Isaiah's words
when the prophet spoke in a taunting-song
 of Babylon's defeated king.
Your Spirit, Loving God, hid in Isaiah's words,
 in his coded mystical meanings about suffering:
"You too have become weak like us,
 you are the same as we."

These words give me comfort, O God,
 for Scripture also says that your son Jesus
was like us in all things but sin,
 sharing our weaknesses and sufferings,
even while fully one with you, O God;
 so you too share my pain.

I find comfort, then, in the cross of Christ,
 upon which was hung all of Earth's suffering.
So I believe, All-Compassionate One,
 that you completely share my human condition,
my weaknesses and even this my pain,
 thus making you both Almighty and All-Weak.

Reflection: *Those who suffer the most are those who suffer alone. However, few truly desire or know how to enter into another's pain and suffering. Compassion is a special holy communion that goes well beyond mere pity or feeling sorry for those suffering. Yet even if you lack truly compassionate companions in your pain this day, you can always find comfort in your compassionate God.*

 Isaiah's words woven into this psalm (see Isaiah 14: 10) are made prophetically true in the Incarnation of Jesus, which proclaims that the Word of God took on human flesh in all its natural weaknesses and suffering. The writer of Hebrews (4: 15) tells us that in the Risen Jesus we have an eternal high priest who can share all our weaknesses and who was tempted in every way we are.

Find comfort, then, in your time of pain and distress not in the Red or Blue Cross but in Christ's Cross.

108

Psalm of the Shattered Cathedral of God
⇒》《⇐

Suffering has shattered my glass cathedral
into ten thousand tiny pieces.
The hammer of pain has smashed the crystal clear God
I had carefully constructed for my comfort.
That heavenly holy prism had made
beautiful rainbows ring-dance round my world.
Now my suffering has smashed it to smithereens.

In my pain I feel Godless, O Divine One,
trying to gather the millions of sacred shreds
of my once crystal pure glass God
to remake meaning of my once perfectly clear world.
My hands become bloodied by the glass
as I struggled to make sense out of my pain
and reglue the shattered pieces of my life.

In my own pain-stained scarlet blood
I see the flowing blood of Christ,
and in this sacred reality I sense
the birthing of a new divine image.

I sense a larger, more encompassing God
than my old God of health and beauty.
Grounded in the pain and cross of Christ,
I start to build a new cathedral,
made of blood and mud, pain and pleasure,
mixing heaven with equal parts of earth.

 Reflection: The God who is worshipped in tidy, clean and flyless holy houses does not fare well when we are struck down by the stormy weather of life. Pain and suffering easily smash to smithereens the purely glass gods of our own making. Pain can create atheists, and it can also create prophetic visionaries of the real God, who is immersed in both awesome beauty and the sacred seamy side of life. Suffering surely brings us to zero gravity, yet it is from that place that we can encounter the One Who Is.

*"Smithereens" comes from the Irish **smidirin**, which means "small fragment." True comfort is to be found in the God of Smithereens, whose concerns encompass a small sparrow falling to earth or a single sun-star — out of the ten billion — that is dying and falling into bottomless space. Find comfort in the midst of your personal pain. Even if it is known only to you, it is also a central concern of your loving God of Smithereens.*

109

Psalm of Groaning, the Name of God
⟫⟪

O my God, forgive my groaning;
I am ashamed not to be able
to silently endure my sufferings,

ashamed that I am not heroic.
And so in my suffering I groan aloud
    to let my body speak its pain.

I groan in my pain and suffering,
    aware that your son Jesus
suffered silently till the very end
    before he cried out in agony.
I feel weak, by Christ's standard, as I groan,
    since my pain is so much less.

Yet, while weak and weary of soul,
    I find great comfort in St. Paul's saying
that your Holy Spirit transforms my inmost groans
    into prayers of pleasing praise
    that reach, O God, to your heart of hearts.
If my groaning can be praise of you,
    then I rejoice in the belief
that groaning is among your holy names.

Reflection: *St. Paul spoke of how in our weakness
we do not know how to pray as we should, and how
the Spirit of God intercedes with inexpressible
groanings that are lovingly understood by God (see
Romans 8: 26). Paul also said that all creation groans in agony
while awaiting the fullness of redemption (Romans 8: 21).*

*Holy groaning is crying out in our pain without shame and
in harmony with the Holy Spirit. The Spirit of Tongues can remake
our groans and sighs into prayers as beautiful as any Alleluia and
lift them up as praise of the God of ten thousand holy names.*

*Once, it is said, a group of the prophet Mohammed's disciples
attempted to silence another disciple who was crying out in great
agony. The holy prophet corrected them, "Let him groan, for
groaning is also one of the names of God."*

*As you suffer, with great reverence release each groan as a
sighing song of praise, for God indeed has many holy names.*

110

A Lost Lover's Psalm

My love was the gravity field
    firmly holding my small world in place,
keeping all the pieces of my life
    securely tied together.
My love was the great magnetic force
    to which work and leisure,
meaning and purpose, clung together as one.

O my Beloved Friend, now my whole world
    is turned suddenly upside down.
For gone is my love, the anchor of my life,
    and I feel so alone, in bed and in life,
adrift in some vast dark sea with no moon;
    gone is the compass of daily routines
that gave direction and substance to my life.

In my pain I reach out toward you, my God,
    to grab your hand as if reaching out
for a fence post in a tornado —
    for I fear you've also fled.
In life my love sometimes overshadowed you,
    and I've never felt your absence so keenly
as now when I've lost the love of my life.

O my God who is Love, let me feel your presence;
    please shout or stamp your feet.
Better yet, hammer on my heart so I will know
    you have not left me too.

Reflection: *The great power of human love to fascinate and engage us can easily seem to eclipse God. Yet God doesn't mind, since God is Love. Tragically, however, the 1-G of love's gravity is destroyed by divorce, a broken friendship, or any love relationship ended by death.*

A God of blessings grounds us in gratitude, and a God of departures challenges us to move on, to pilgrimage toward new loves and a new relationship with God. Separation from those we deeply loved is truly painful; it can cast us into the zero gravity of loneliness, regret and deep dejection. Yet in the process of grief, along our lonely pilgrimage of pain, we can emigrate to a new homeland. There the zero gravity of loss, like all true poverty of spirit, becomes a blessing because at its core there is love. With eyes of love we can see that what appeared to be an eclipse of God was only a faint passing thin cloud illuminated by the sun.

God of blessings and of disappointments,
God of abundant love and of broken hearts,
be with us always.

111

Psalm for a Deceased Mother
❖❖❖

O God from whose womb we have all come,
    my mother and I were one when as an infant
I lived within her, drawing on her life and love
    until the day we were separated.
She birthed me, and severed was the cord
    that linked us in intimate love.

Now death has cut the cord of life
    that has united her and me.

Intertwined in the womb and in life,
    we are now separated,
but I find a sign of hope
    in the center of my body.

May I see my navel as a holy birthmark,
    a sacred sign that in both life and death
we are forever connected
    through the Cord of Life.
As once joined on earth, so now in heaven.

May this blessed birth cord woven on heaven's loom,
    stronger than death's sharp knife,
tether me forever to my mother
    and to you, the Source of all Life.

May the birth pangs of dying
    be for her not an Eden curse but a blessing
    that purifies her of all human failings.
May her sins be forgiven
    and her motherly love rewarded.

Reflection: *The connection between a mother and her child is a stronger, more primal bond than any other relationship. It is so intimate since mother and child have shared the same body, the same blood and life fluids. The deepest love, fed by the most profound dependence and the most profound nurturance, flows back and forth along the cord that connects mother and child. While the death of all loved ones is deeply mourned, uniquely poignant is the death of one's mother.*

This psalm-prayer can be recited at the time of your mother's death, on your mother's death anniversary, on your mother's birth-date or even on your birthday. You might add to this psalm the visual prayer of lovingly gazing at your navel as you prayerfully remember your mother.

112

Psalm for a Deceased Father

Our Father who art in heaven,
    bless my father now with you.
Divine Father, bless him for his efforts
    to love me as you love me.
I am the flower of his love for my mother,
    the child of his seed.
With pride, I find his fingerprints
    in my body, mind and heart.

I remember his strong love for me
    penned not in poems,
but written in the sweat of his hard work
    to clothe, feed and shelter me from storm.
As I recall his many sacrifices in life,
    I carry his family name with pride.

O God whom we call our Father,
    bless my beloved father, who guided my growth,
who set me straight when I took a wrong turn,
    who even in his shortcomings
was an image of you in his care for me;
    may he now be in heaven, resting in you,
held in your strong embrace forever.

Reflection: *While we usually think of the primal biological unity that binds together a mother and her child, a primal unity of love also binds a father to his children. This cord, which was begun in lovemaking and seeded with sperm is woven into an unbreakable lovecord by years of hard work, self-sacrifice, protection and care. It has a divine strength since its weaving has been overseen by angels.*

This paternal cord of love links forever a father and his child.

Regardless of our parents' failings and faults, it is our solemn duty to remember them with prayer and gratitude. It is wise to withhold any judgment of our parents until we have had children and raised them to adulthood. Only then do we catch more than glimmers of understanding about how our parents tried to be the very best parents they could be. Until we have that full insight, we need to hold on to the best and strongest strands of our relationship with our parents as we hold them in prayer before God.

As with the previous psalm for a deceased mother, this psalm-prayer can be recited at the time of your father's death, on your father's death anniversary, on your father's birthdate or even on your birthday.

113

Psalm Song for a Dead Friend
-»»·«««-

O God, whom I call my Friend,
    tears choke at my throat
as I sing this love song
    for my dear dead friend.

Inspire me to sing of our love
    to the melody of memories
in the times of love we shared,
    a reflection, my God, of your love for us.

I sing now in death what once
    I only could write in letters:
"My dearest friend"
    and "I love you."

This love song to my friend
　　　has no final crashing chord,
nor does our friendship,
　　　which is forever one
in you our God who is Love.

 Reflection: *God is Love, and of that we have good Gospel proof. Faith in that truth should open our eyes to see that, in God, the love of friendship is not second class to married love. In our society, love in friendship is only considered proper if it is restrained. Like mild chili, only tempered love friendships — whether among those of the same or opposite sex — are thought to be safe to stomach.*

While our letters still often begin with the greeting "Dear" — or even, "My dear" — such terms of endearment dare not be spoken naked off paper. This psalm challenges us to cross beyond our culture's limiting boundaries and emigrate to the zero-gravity land of love-within-friendship, where the word "dear" need not be a frosting word since it is spoken with a full heart and soul.

Friend *is a sacred name, to be used with great care. It requires us to separate those who are only business associates and acquaintances from real friends. If you have even one or two truly good friends, then you are blessed.*

While this psalm is included among those for the dead, praying it before the death of a friend can help free you from regret at the friend's death. You might even dare bridging the canyon of culture, saying to your friend today what one day you may wish you had said: "I love you, dear."

II. Psalms of Lamentation

Lamentations in the First Testament take various forms, one of which is poem-songs of grief at the time of death. These dirges were sung by relatives or even by professional mourners. The prophets often made use of the lamentation style of prayer when describing the defeat of nations or peoples.

Lamentations were also personal psalm-prayers in which the petitioner cried out in pain over various personal misfortunes. About one third of the Psalms of David are lamentations that sing of misfortune and great distress.

The title of lamentations also refers to the Hebrew Scriptures that speak of the desolation of Jerusalem or of those who have been struck down by God's anger. At times these poem-prayers are prophetic, and often they deal with a crisis of faith.

The following psalm-poems of lamenting provide a Second Testament perspective on times of great grieving and sorrow. Because of a belief in the resurrection, Christians too often feel guilty about lamenting.

Today's theological stress upon the joy of the resurrection has sadly sometimes made expressions of grieving and tears appear to be a sign of a lack of faith in the promise of life after death. To be sure, resurrection joy is at the core of Christian faith. Yet we must not underestimate the profound effect of the zero gravity of grief in our lives. May the following psalms of lamentation provide a prayer expression for those of us who see death as both an occasion for belief in the resurrection and a time of great personal loss and deep sorrow.

114

The Wailing Psalm

I want to wail and scream in pain,
 and not wash my face or comb my hair.
I want to fast from food and drink,
 to abstain from music and fun.
I want to kick the walls and beat my breast,
 and even tear out the telephone.
I'd throw away my mail and speak to no one,
 but I am ashamed to grieve.

O God, how can I ever be the same again
 or feel the earth solidly beneath my feet,
for ripped to shreds are all my daily rituals,
 my patterns of living, loving and sharing.
My heart feels full not of blood but of pain,
 my lungs filled with screams, not breath.
My eyes are blinded to all by my bitter tears,
 but I am ashamed of my lack of Easter hope.

O God, I know how you felt
 on that terrible Good Friday.
So I ask you to say nothing to me now,
 for nothing can be said.
Only hold me in your love, O God,
 till the pain passes, if it ever will.
And pardon, I pray, my feeble faith
 as I mourn like one without hope.

Reflection: *Grief at a great loss — like the death of a beloved, a life companion, a child or a parent — should not be expressed in middle-class moderation. Our religious faith in the promise of eternal life*

given by Jesus should not seal our lips from singing dirges.

Death is a surgery without anesthesia. The radical loss of what cannot be replaced is not to be taken lightly. Our Jewish religious heritage prescribed physical displays of mourning which signaled to others that life was not going on as usual. That wisdom proclaimed the need to mourn by casting dirt on one's head, leaving one's hair uncombed, fasting from food and entertainment and all tokens of joy, slapping one's body, wearing old garments and walking barefoot. Yet even if our mourning finds a more contemporary expression, healthy grieving after a death helps heal the lost part of ourselves. It helps us acclimate to the zero gravity of loss, at the center of which lives hope in the promise of God.

115

A Psalm of Despair
❧≫≪❧

O my God, how am I to go on, tell me?
        How am I to again take up my work,
chatting casually about the weather,
        talking about today's sports scores
or enjoying a discussion about the evening news,
        when the one I've loved is dead?

How am I to smile and say "Thank you"
        to those with sad voices who say,
"You have my sympathy, I am sorry" —
        how can I keep from screaming?
For sympathy does not heal my pain;
        sympathy doesn't bring back the dead.

O God, how can I not stuff my ears shut

to polite words of condolence
by those now safe from death's sting,
    from whom death has stolen no one?
How do I respond to flowers and kind notes
    sent by those responding from social shoulds,
rather than from the pit of pain?

As Jesus raised Lazarus from the tomb,
    raise me, O God, from the pit of pity,
that I might respond in honest love,
    graciously receiving all who seek to console,
who comfort me with cumbersome kindness.

Reflection: *Death is a thief that robs the tongue of words that have meaning. Death is a presence we prefer to avoid, a naked presence so uncomfortable that we seek to escape from it as soon as politely possible. We stumble, not knowing what to say when we attempt to express our regrets, especially when the one who has died was not close to us. We use the secondhand language of religious expressions, vacant of faith and meaning, cliches that are threadbare from overuse.*

Mindful of this, when we join others in mourning, we should do so with great reverence and care. At the tomb of his good friend Lazarus, Jesus did not console his friend's sisters; he wept. Tears, when honest and real, say what tongues cannot express.

And when we receive expressions of sympathy, we need to be generous in accepting gifts of condolence, graciously deaf to those whose expressions of sorrow are weak or self-centered. Our beloved who has died, not to mention God, would want us to act in no other way than with generous and gracious love.

116

The Fingerprints of Grief Psalm
⇒⟫⟪⇐

O God who loves rich variety,
    who created not simply a single tree,
but trees of all kinds, sizes and shapes,
    let me see the vast variety in ways of mourning.
Grant me the grace never to judge others
    in how or how long they grieve.

As unique as human fingerprints,
    so varied and different are the ways
each of us grieves and mourns
    the loss of one so greatly loved.
Gift me with the grace, O God who holds us all,
    not to compare my sorrow
with the anguish of others who share my loss.

May I never compare grief, O God,
    or judge the apparent absence of mourning,
the seeming excess of tears
    or the length of time it takes to heal.
Only grant that my wound dealt by death
    may become glorious as the wounds of Christ.

Reflection: *The ways of lamenting the loss of someone we love are as unique and different as finger- and soul-prints. In the midst of our great sorrow, this psalm calls us to remember that external signs of mourning are not grief gauges for judging the degree to which others may have loved the deceased.*

For some, mourning may be an underground river, and for others a cascading waterfall of tearful grief. We all need to be natural, and we need to be compassionately non-judgmental of others in our family who mourn differently.

We need to be sensitive in contacts with those who are mourning on the inside, perhaps months and months following the death of a spouse, child, parent or dear friend. Our society's assembly-line mentality of "Let's get back to business as soon as possible" requires many to mourn in disguise. Love calls us to be sensitive to all who have been visited by death.

117

Psalm of the Communion of Sorrow

O Compassionate God,
    hear my soul's sad lament.
I am ashamed that my sorrow
    is itself so sorry,
so seemingly inferior and worthless.

Heal my poor words of sympathy
    when I say "I'm sorry,"
for they are so limp and sickly,
    disconnected from real pain,
safely distant from personal suffering.

Any true communion of sorrow
    involves feeling sick myself,
suffering another's anguish,
    pain, sickness and loss.
Grant me, O God,
    a measure of such compassion.

My Beloved, give me the gift

not so much to be patient
with those who are suffering
but to be *a* patient
who suffers with the suffering.

 Reflection: *The ability to be in communion with those who are suffering loss, sickness or misfortune is not a human but a divine talent. Sadly, expressions of polite sorrow are often sorry, devoid of any sharing in the other's suffering.*

When we first encounter another's suffering, an authentic compassionate anguish usually arises within us. However, if the suffering or sickness is extended over several days or longer, the suffering one often becomes a "pain." It is then that we especially need to pray for the divine gift of compassion, particularly if the victim of sickness, suffering or loss is someone with whom we live or work. At such times we need to pray that we can live in a holy communion of compassion so we can share the person's pain.

This psalm could be a daily prayer for those who minister to the sick. It can be a prayer for anyone caring for an elderly or sick family member. When spoken with a full heart and with a desire to drink as deeply as possible of the other's pain and suffering, we might simply say the beautiful three-word prayer, "I am sorry."

118

The String of Life Psalm
⇛⇚

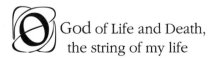 God of Life and Death,
the string of my life

is running out,
>   and I know the end is near.
Only now can I see
>   how little I've wanted you.
Awaken me before I die,
>   O Lord of Life and Death.

With a pawnshop owner's eyes
>   I see that all of it is trash,
everything I valued greatly:
>   the luxuries and conveniences,
all my IRAs and saving accounts,
>   my treasures under lock and key.
All these I wanted more than you,
>   the only treasure of any value.
Still, now, Lord, fire up the furnace
>   of my cool, half-hungry heart.

I rejoice in my sage, aged eyes,
>   since senior years see more.
For love ripens fully with age,
>   making senior love richer.
So, my God, let's you and I make love.

Reflection: Senior citizen romances have their own flavor, and they proclaim that falling in love is not only for the youthful. Many famous saints seem to have fallen head over heels in love with God in their late teens. Yet, don't feel regret if in your youth or middle years you were too busy to lose your balance and fall helplessly in love with God. Only heaven knows how joyfully crowded with unknown, saintly senior lovers is the zero-gravity world of the kingdom.

Elder lovers are often better lovers, not because they have more leisure time but because they have more insight. Years give them the eyes of pawnshop owners able to correctly judge what is truly valuable and what is trash. And God is swept away in delight *whenever a long-loved lover suddenly awakens to God's passionate love and finally comes a'courting.*

Since none of us knows how much of life's invisible ball of string is left for us, senior lovers can be anyone from age 18 to 108. Blessed are those who are never too old to fall in love.

119

The Psalm of Passing On
⟫ ⟪

Such an obscene expression: "to die" —
the polite never utter aloud
such vulgar, grave, dirty words.
Neighbors do not die, they pass on;
friends and family do not die, they pass away.

"Died" is an ugly period-word
that ends a sentence.
It closes the door with a slam,
seals the tomb.
Yet in this "passing on" avoidance
is found a mystical truth.

For death is the great passage,
a passing beyond sickness
and the valley of disappointment,
a passage through the womb of the tomb,
a passage over life's limitations.

Since death is for you, O God of the Passover,
a voyage of returning,
a joyous triumphant homecoming,

help me the next time I'm told
that acquaintances have "passed on,"
    not to cringe, but to smile
and to say, "Ah, yes, they have indeed."

 Reflection: *In modern society, the disowning of death is another way of reinforcing normal gravity. So powerful is our avoidance that even when death visits as close as our door, the magnetic force of our denial pulls us away from reality. In a short time after the death of someone close, we forget the specter of death and fall into the drugged slumber of those who believe they will not die any time soon.*

When absolutely forced to relate to death, we search for words that attempt to remove the sting of death and that blind us to its fearful nearness. Paradoxically, if we believe that in death there is a rebirth, then to die is truly to "pass on," to simply pass from this life to the next. While the implications of that folk expression may be unconscious, the words can lead to a powerful reflection on death. In the language of school, to "pass" implies successfully completing an examination or moving from one level of education to another. The rich religious term Passover offers another slant on the subject of death, one that implies liberation and promise.

120

The Angels of Gethsemani Psalm
⋙⋘

I lift up my heart to you,
    O God of all comfort,
thankful for the presence of friends

and my caring family
as I wrestle with death.

I am grateful for them,
      for their prayer and presence,
for their solace and support,
      as I climb onto my cross
in these last hours of my life.

I lift up my heart to you, my God,
      for you have given me these people
to help transform my Good Friday
      into another holy Easter
crowded with hope and promise.

I feel blessed by the gifts
      of their time and care
generously given to me
      as I now lie dying
on my Calvary hilltop.

Thank you for sending to me
      in my friends and family
not just one Angel of Gethsemani
      but a heavenly crowd
to comfort me in my dying hours.

 Reflection: *Death and isolated suffering are our greatest enemies and oppressors; on the cross even Jesus felt abandoned by God. Yet our compassionate God shares the agony of our zero gravity of anguish. God hears the cries of the poor and oppressed, the sick and the dying. At a deathbed, God's presence can easily be read with braille touch, for the fingerprints of God are on each card and gift of flowers, in each tangible expression of love and concern by others.*

The Sacrament of the Sick is more than a priestly use of blessed oil and the saying of prayers as death draws near. It's

completed by the holy sacraments of the presence and love of others. Blessed are those who administer such holy sacraments to the dying. Blessed are those who are surrounded by love and prayer as they die to this life and are born into another.

This psalm-prayer could be prayed by one who is dying or recited by a family member if the dying person is unable to read it.

121

The Psalm of Dying
➔➤✕《《✕

ike a poor old bent nail, O God,
    I am being pulled
by the great magnet of your love,
    and I'm ready to let go of this life
to come racing home to you.

Beloved, this old rusty nail hangs taut,
    torn between you and my loved ones,
those who do not want me to die,
    who would have me remain with them
and not go flying off to you.

Suspended, I am spinning in space
    between two gravity fields
pulling me in opposite directions.
    As St. Paul said, this old nail
is caught between two worlds,
    between home and Home.

Send your holy carpenter-son, Jesus,
    not to hammer me deeper into this life,

but to pull me up and out
    of the old wood of this world
and to lift me up to you.

May those I love not mourn long
    the empty hole I leave behind,
but let them fill it full with memories
    till they too are lifted up to you.

 Reflection: *St. Paul wrote beautifully of the twin mystical magnets that held him dangling between two loves. He longed to depart in death from this life and be home with Christ; at the same time he felt the obligation-pull to remain on Earth for the sake of those who would benefit from his presence (see Philippians 1: 21-24).*

Similarly, it's not uncommon for a dying person to experience a longing to be with God, a yearning to finish the painful struggle of hanging on to this life. At the same time, the dying can feel the intense magnetism of family and loved ones clinging to them out of love and/or need.

The dying can also be held bed-bound by an unwritten cultural code or spiritual obligation that says one must struggle to hold on to life till the bitter end, and so they may feel guilty for wanting to depart this life. Family and friends must sometimes transform their attachment to the dying person into a longing for the loved one's liberation in God.

To let go of one who is deeply loved, allowing the loved one to die, requires faith that death is not the end but only a transition point in life. It also requires a belief that anyone or anything we love in life is only loaned to us for a very brief time. We need to embrace those who are dying with both affection and the permission to return to God. Giving these twin gifts of love, we help them have a happy death.

Blessed are those who frequently offer back to God that which is only entrusted to them for a short while, for they shall never feel robbed at the time of death.

III. Psalms of Regret and Repentance

"Repent, for the reign of God has come" — this was the message of Jesus of Galilee. For centuries his original words in Aramaic were translated as "Do penance" rather than "Repent." This rendering helped craft a Christian spirituality of hairshirts, long fasts and physical denial. Harsh penances that train the body to be subject to the spirit are found in many world religions. Jesus does not promote this kind of spiritual discipline, but rather proclaims a practice of *returning*, which is implied in the original word *repent*.

Repenting is the opposite of sinning, which is a type of emigration, a running away from home to find delight in whatever promises joy and pleasure. Sin is the result of being pulled away from God by the gravity of something that wears a mask of Godlike pleasure. Soon the mask is dropped, and the sinner finds her/himself to be in exile.

Yet exile creates homesickness and the longing to return. Some of the most beautiful poetry and psalms express the bittersweet pain of this longing to return again to the Beloved. Morbid guilt over violating some law or the fear of punishment due to an offense have never given birth to great poetry or music, but an ardent desire to return to God has inspired masterpieces.

To repent means more than a change in attitude or a reversal in one's behavior; it is a return to a love relationship. Along with sorrow for our turning away from God, a return from exile begins with the profound belief that God laments, more than we, our departure and resulting separation. God's steadfast love continues to invite us home to love again.

The following prayer-psalms are intended to assist us in this primal religious passion to return from exile.

122

The Emery Stone Angel Psalm

O God, send me your angel
    with heaven's emery stone
to sharpen my dull conscience
    now gone painlessly blunt.

I lament how I no longer feel,
    as I did in years gone by,
when its sharp spurs dug deeply
    into my tender, throbbing heart.

Those whirling pinpricks of love
    would prod me to seek forgiveness
as soon as I'd rudely wound a dear one,
    thus keeping my love alive.

Angel of God, grind its edges
    sharp as razor blades
so I can feel its alarming sting
    and thus not cause pain to my Beloved.

Reflection: The Arizona Native American Indians speak of the conscience as a little three-cornered object in the heart that stands still when we are good. When we are bad, it furiously whirls around in a circle, causing acute irritation. If we continue doing bad, however, the corners eventually wear down and the discomfort ceases to be felt.

Nothing is so dangerous to lovers as a smooth-cornered conscience. Dulled by time and lack of attention, a blunted conscience no longer irritates us when we are rude, self-centered or ungrateful. Young lovers, being right in the throes of love, have sharp three-cornered objects which whirl wildly in their hearts at the slightest neglect or injury. Their consciences thus send them racing to ask forgiveness for causing pain.

Our physical survival prods us to frequently test the batteries in our smoke alarms. Similarly, frequent testing of the sharpness of the three-cornered consciences in our hearts is a necessity for our survival as lovers. Paradoxically, the further along we travel on the path to God, the sharper the edges of our consciences need to become. When have you last tested the alertness of your conscience?

123

Psalm of A Lover's Lament

My dear God, forgive me!
　　I ask your pardon
not because I disobeyed a law
　　or broke a commandment
but for my sinful, foolish rudeness.

You and I were intertwined,
　　dancing together
to the music of our hearts,
　　and I abandoned you
to go dancing on my own.

It was not you I held but me —
　　clutching myself with glee
as I waltzed to the music
　　of my narrow needs and wants,
blindly ignoring you, Lord of the Dance.

Dear God, come and kiss me
   with your pardon.
Encircle me in your love
   as I dare to ask:
Would you care to dance?

 Reflection: *Many are the temptations to stray from the homeward road we travel as pilgrims returning to God. Equally numerous are the occasions to repent and return.*

Yet this returning to God is more than a journey; it is a dance, since all the way home to God is part of an intimate love affair with God. To sin is indeed to become lost on our way by choosing a wrong road, but perhaps sin is more like forgetting with whom we are dancing.

When our relationship with God is a matter of obedience to divine laws and regulations, then relief, not rejoicing, is the result of repentance! Indeed, it's a great solace that pardon relieves the fear that our actions have separated us from one we love. But the joy of love restored should tower over our relief.

124

The Public Sinner Psalm
⇥⇤

O God, sin seems so private and personal,
   so I struggle to see my corporate sin,
my part of the human family's failure to love you.

As I prepare to confess my trespasses and faults,

remind me that we are one Body,
and so we all share in an unholy communion of sin.

O God, cleanse your people, of whom I am one;
    remove our sins of neglect and abuse,
forgive our injustices and social sins.

I heartily regret all the sins of my society
    and my personal share
in our collective actions and attitudes
    of discrimination, violence and disregard for life.

Lord, have mercy on me for my global sins,
    for in Christ we are one Body,
a Body comprised of both saints and sinners all.

 Reflection: *Social and global sin, the sin in which all people share, is the most difficult to acknowledge and then confess. Even a casual glance at social evils like racial hatred, religious discrimination, genocide and ethnic cleansing makes it difficult to deny public sin. Moreover, the twentieth century has witnessed how entire nations and their churches have participated in the ugly sin of segregation.*

We share in public and global sin to the degree of our personal involvement, and that involvement extends to our words and attitudes. We also participate by our silence and our failure to denounce or confront social evil. Perhaps no other century in history has witnessed such horrible global sins as the twentieth century. Those of us who have lived in a time of such massive murder by genocide and exploitation of the poor cannot easily dismiss the need to ask for forgiveness for our personal share in national and international sins.

125

The Procrastinator Psalm
⇒⟩⟩ ⟨⟨⇐

Forgive me, my Beloved Friend,
    for I procrastinate,
ever postponing till tomorrow
    any personal conversion,
any real reform of my life.

Forgive me, for I love my habits
    more than I love you.
I prefer my old daily ruts
    to traveling the new roads
to becoming a new person in Christ.

I prophylactically protect myself
    with my pious prayers
that comfort me in my life
    of holy compromise
instead of embracing your message
    of reform and radical change.

Pardon first of all my procrastination,
    the enabler of all my other sins,
and give me the penance to live each day
    as if it were the day of my death,
so I can become serious about converting
    the root sins that really need reform.

Reflection: *Confession of faults is a common religious practice. While significant sins or failures in life can invoke true sorrow and repentance, the confession of faults is usually more a custom than a true conversional cleansing! We procrastinate at doing what really*

needs to be done: changing our hearts and minds according to the zero-gravity pattern of the Gospel. We reinforce this procrastination by focusing our attention on lesser faults. Minor failings to pray daily or attend Sunday worship and such sins as gossip and vulgar language are camouflaged confessions that conceal instead of reveal what truly needs reforming.

Camouflage is French for blowing smoke into someone's face. The pious confession of sins at a revival or in the sacrament of reconciliation can often be blowing holy smoke in God's face. As a disciple of the Great Reformer, Jesus, pray this psalm and then consider smoking your root sins out from their holes. Consider, for example, taking a minor failing like uncharitable speech and following it back to its source sin. Dig down deep and see if envy, pride, jealousy or some other serious sin might be at the root. Such sins that can insidiously control our lives are the ones to expose to our awareness, repentance and the mercy of God. Don't put off addressing such root sins. Ask the God of all prodigal sons and daughters to open the eyes of your soul to see besides the dust of daily failings, the hidden evil of your real sins.

126

Psalm of My Encore Sin
⟫⟪

My God, I regret to confess
my old encore sin,
which, alas, I have committed again.
I am ashamed to confess
that I've slipped and fallen again
into my old sinful pattern.

I feel like Pavlov's dancing dog,
　　making constant curtain calls
with my tired old act,
　　which isn't funny anymore.
Since you are my perpetual audience,
　　my encore sinning must weary you.

O Loving, Forgiving God, help me
　　to discover the traps into which I fall
before I look up from the bottom of the pit,
　　the traps that cause me to endlessly encore
my sad act (＿＿*acknowledge your encore sin*＿＿).

Grant that with your grace, my God,
　　I can instead make
good works and loving you
　　the encore which I love to do
　　again and again and again.

 Reflection: *Overcoming encore sinning, committing the same failings, especially the low-grade, common household variety sins, is the challenge of the truly repentant. Big sins that shock even seasoned confessors are rarely the stuff of confession. Our favorite encore sins are the ones that should bring us to our knees asking the forgiveness of God. They should also bring us to the feet of those we love and live with, who must suffer from the effects of these sins.*

Alcoholism and drug use are not the only sins of addiction. There are a host of other sins of habit that can become misery-go-rounds for ourselves and for those with whom we live and work. These frequently repeated sins are made possible by the failure to sandpaper our consciences, making them tender to the touch. A dull conscience makes it easy to keep our patterns of causing recurring pain.

127

The Regretter Psalm

I regret, O God, and moan my sad lament
    at failing again and again
to see you, my beautiful, wonderful Lover,
    at the many intersections of my daily life.

I am sorry I stumble so blindly past you,
    my ears and eyes so often clogged shut,
cluttered with my tinkertoy agendas,
    preoccupied with my mosquito-sized trials.

I regret not being intoxicatingly drunk on you
    in all I see, in everything around me.
I'm saddened by my failure to acknowledge you, O God,
    as I pause now to open my eyes
to how I have so often neglected your visitations:
    (*pause for silent reflection*).

My Beloved and Generous God,
    I repent of all my sins of blindness
to your daily thousand-and-one visits
    and all the countless gifts you send my way.

Reflection: *Regret can be a repeated response to life, a pervasive pattern. Few of us do not know its sting. We can regret acts that are wrong and sinful, and we can regret failing to do good. We can also regret failing to acknowledge the presence of God.*

Aging often brings a flood of regrets for missed opportunities and aborted dreams, for talent-gifts left unwrapped and for roads not taken. Yet when the Way becomes a Lover's Lane, regretting can become a romantic awakening.

Like all repentance, healthy regret can bring us to the blessed zero gravity of the Gospel. As a spiritual discipline, frequent regretting — the kind marked out in this psalm — can work miracles. It can give sight to the blind, hearing to the deaf and speech and song to the mute. Doing the inner work of facing our regrets now can also lead to great blessing. For blessed are those who die a happy death, a death that's left regrets behind.

Chapter 7

Space Station Psalms

 Zero gravity is a fact of life both for astronauts circling our planet Earth and for adventurers who will someday live in stations on the moon or in space. Those who pray the prayers of this book may themselves never be emigrants from planet Earth who live aboard space stations. The following prayers, however, can provide an extra-global perspective on life, and on Earth, for those still earthbound.

Spacecraft and space stations that one day become homes for colonies of people from planet Earth will by necessity have very limited space. There will not be room for various Christian churches on every corner, or for scattered mosques, synagogues and temple shrines. Earth's emigrants will be fortunate to have a single room or section for religious worship.

This will necessitate the forging of a yet-undiscovered communion among Earth's religious traditions which honors each without the unreligious attitude of each one seeking to dominate. The real zero gravity of outer space may require letting go of our earthbound insistence on the exclusive rightness of our particular religious expression. Countless questions might arise in bringing about such a communion of religions, like the name given to this common worship room or whether it has any sacred images and, if so, what kind.

The emigration into space might repeat the American experiments of freedom *of* religion and freedom *from* religion — experiments that still are in process at the start of the third millennium of the common era. Emigrants who settled North America sought to escape religious wars, persecutions and discrimination by those of whatever religious group dominated their native land. These emigrants to America carried their unique religious traditions, customs and practices to their new land and attempted to maintain and pass them on to their children.

Unfortunately the suitcases of these emigrants also contained all their old prejudices and hates. Perhaps the luggage and hearts of all those who will emigrate from Earth should be inspected so that space isn't polluted with our intolerance of different cultures, religions and races. It's to be hoped that those future emigrants from Earth will create a new model for a common expression of God that takes into account both the successes and the failures of the American experiment.

As a new millennium begins, the future of space stations has been predominately the concern of science and technology, while religions seem unconcerned. Reports back to Earth from the earliest spacecraft explorers have spoken of almost every aspect of human life except two, sex and religion. While the first is sure to soon become a part of life in space, the second, religion, may depend not so much on God as upon us! Religious people of all faiths today who reject and refuse to explore any real respectful communion among religious expressions should look at the possible serious and far-reaching consequences of such an attitude.

I. Holy Variety:
Psalms of Religious Communion

With our religious roots intertwined, we ascend on the wings of compassion to the unity of the Divine Mystery, the All Holy One, the Unnameable.

The thought of Earth's emigrants living and praying together in space in peace and harmony could be considered impossible based on our ageless history of religious division and discrimination. Yet, unless those presently gravity-bound by narrow attitudes are willing to strive to find some holy variety in our expressions of prayer, then God and religion may be forever bound by the gravity of this small planet.

The psalms of this next section are an effort to help build a mutual appreciation and a communion of praise among some of the rich traditions of Earth's religions that have been inspired by God's Spirit.

128

Psalm of the True Believer
-≫-≪-

O Holy One, you must weep
       as you look from above
at our poor wounded world,
       scared and scourged,
bruised black and blue
       by religious wars
waged against unbelievers
       by the righteous faithful
of all Earth's religions.

The view from outer space
       sees a battered planet,
Earth bruised and bloodied
       by those with a "holy" license
to hate, despise and kill
       anyone of another belief —
and who do so in your holy name.

Millenniums of holy wars
       and wounds gorged red
and deeper than grand canyons,
       can never be removed
simply by words of mild regret
       from lips that refuse to seek
true holy communion.

Only true believers can hope
       to heal and to restore
the primal pristine unity
       of the Body of the Holy One,
the vision, O Boundless God,
       of your holy and earthen family
being truly brothers and sisters.

I strive to be a true believer
       and daily bow before you,
professing my four-word creed,
       "I believe in God."
I daily do my best to keep
       your one and only law,
your commandment to love.

 Reflection: *Once the holy prophet Mohammed was asked to tell what makes one a true believer, and he replied, "If you find great pleasure in the good you do and are grieved by the evil which you*

do, then you are a true believer." Judaism likewise teaches, "I say to you: Deeds of love are worth as much as all the commandments of the law."

Contradicting the ancient caste system of the East — in which the accident of birth makes a Brahmin holy or an outcast unclean — Buddhism teaches: "No Brahmin is a Brahmin by birth. No outcast is an outcast by birth. An outcast is an outcast by his/her deeds. A Brahmin is a Brahmin by his/her deeds."

For Christians of countless varieties, Jesus speaks the same inclusive truth of God. He said we will know others' religion by the fruit of their lives, not by the name they call their tree: "By their fruits you shall know them" (see Matthew 7: 17-20).

True believers, while taking pride in their religious tradition, struggle daily to live out the largest implications of their beliefs, often moving beyond the narrow views and practices their religion fosters.

129

The Seed Sowing Psalm
➤➤❯❮❮❮

O Divine Mystery, assist me
　　to be a wise gardener,
who, with great care, will sow
　　only good seeds this day,
those deeds and attitudes
　　that truly will give you glory.

If by habit, sloth or accident,
　　I might sow an evil seed,
in haste, before it takes root,

may I pluck it up at once,
lest it grow an evil harvest.

Every word, deed and hidden thought
is a seed whose DNA insures
a fruit unfolding to ripe maturity
that someday will be
my life-harvest returned to me.

May it be, O Holy One, a harvest of Life.

 Reflection: *Hinduism teaches the universal law of harvesting: "You cannot gather what you did not sow." The Sikh sages of India echo this law of the Holy One and of nature: "Whatever people sow, that shall they reap. If they sow trouble, then trouble will be their harvest. If they sow poison, they cannot expect ambrosia." Buddhism likewise warns us, "It is nature's rule that as we sow, so shall we reap." St. Paul in Galatians (6: 7) repeats this teaching when he says, "A person will reap only what he sows." Jesus himself tells us, "The measure with which you measure will be measured back to you" (Mark 4: 24), to which Confucius chimes in, "What proceeds from you will return to you."*

It seems strange that such a universal religious teaching is not placed at the top of the daily list of religious disciplines. The prime directive for all peoples should be, "Sow only good seeds. Never sow evil."

As you go about your duties today, exercise the greatest care in everything you say, do and think so that your tomorrows will find your life-barns overflowing with a harvest of good.

How many centuries of careful sowing of justice, peace, harmony and goodness will it take for the people on planet Earth to reverse the horrible harvest of violence, hate and evil sown for millenniums in the name of religion by all peoples?

130

The Unsayable Psalm
❧❧ ❦❦

O Unspeakable One of Endless Ages,
    teach me how to speak
that great forgotten wordless language
    so my love can sing to you.

Mere words cannot create
    a song whose melody
captures heart and soul.

Just as unsayable are you, Divine One,
    whose melody is the mystery
that captivates my soul with love.

May I be joyfully tongue-tied, Beloved,
    to live my love
as a wordless song to you.

Reflection: *"The subtle truth of the universe is unsayable and unthinkable" is a fundamental Taoist principle recorded in the* **Hua Hu Ching**, *the book of Lao Tzu's unknown teachings. Taoism is the religion of ancient China flowing from this mystic teacher who taught that direct experience is the way to know the Divine Mystery.*

Lao Tzu's insight echoes the spiritual awareness of the Jewish people for whom the very name of God is unsayable. This holy global wisdom needs a resurrection in an age of information that produces a daily deluge of data. Silence is a Noah's Ark to ride out the flood of noise and chatter. It is especially necessary when addressing what is beyond words.

Unspeakable! The bloated human mind, in both secular and sacred circles, rebels at the idea of anything being unspeakable,

unthinkable, indescribable or indefinable, even the Divine Mystery.
The human tongue prides itself in vast vocabularies that can express
every emotion and thought and can even speak the language of
God.

Besides incorporating the wisdom of Lao Tzu, the above psalm
refers to Thomas Wolfe's wonderful line in **Look Homeward**
Angel*, "Remembering speechlessly we seek the great forgotten*
language." Praying in the forgotten language is so simple as to be
done without effort, yet it is also very difficult. How hard it is for
us simply to be. To pray in the forgotten language is to be still, to
silently hold a space of awe in the face of the splendor of the
universe in all its brilliance or the beautiful bloom of a single
flower.

Silence allows us to be in the Presence. Soak up the Presence
until your heart is full to overflowing, then let your tongueless
heart sing the long forgotten language of your love.

Silent wonder introduces us to a unique sense of zero gravity.
It is the most ecumenical and global of all prayer — both on
Earth and perhaps someday in space.

131

Psalm of the Hungry Mystery
⇒》》《《⇐

To what can I compare you, O Holy Mystery;
    is there on earth or in the heavens
anything to which you can be likened?

I cannot find an adequate image
    to feed my ever hungry mind.
So I ask: Shall I name you a Holy Nothing,
    like an invisible energy radiating nothing,

some dark, mystical black hole?

Each year, the black holes in space
    effortlessly swallow
millions of giant sun-stars larger than ours,
    as they vanish forever
into the massive mystery of magnetic Nothingness.

Scholars wonder whether each galaxy's heart
    may contain a black hole,
an invisible whirlpool tunnel
    possessing all known gravity,
allowing nothing, neither time nor space
    to escape its voracious appetite.

O Holy Mystery, are you such a dark womb,
    invisible to the eye and the most sensitive scope?
Are you a Cosmic Lover drawing everything to yourself
    in a passionate desire
to consume all in a total communion?
    If so, my God, all I need do is let go.

Reflection: *All God-talk is based on some earthly comparison or analogy. Images of God are rooted in human experience, thus making the Divine Reality in some way accessible to our experience. At the same time, any image puts human limits on the Mystery we call God.*

This psalm offers the insight that it is not we who go in search of the Holy Mystery. Rather, regardless of whether the Mystery is called God, Allah, I Am, or by any other name, it is the Unspeakable Mystery that draws us. Like a devouring black hole, it seeks to sweep us up into itself.

Such an invisible, imageless image of the Divine can make us aware of our profound lack of gravity in relation to God and can be a bridge for communion with the wisdom of those religions that condone no images of the Divine One.

132

Psalm of the Secret Monk and Nun

y habit, my religious robes, O Holy One,
    are the common daily clothes I wear.

My monastery and my cell, O Mystery,
    are my work space and my home.

My prayer bell is the telephone,
    calling me to temporal times of prayer.

My three vows are charity, charity
    and more charity, for all.

Reflection: *Life itself is the spiritual life of the follower of the Chinese Tao tradition. In the **Hua Hu Ching** (number 47), Lao Tzu teaches that "Chanting is no more holy than listening to the murmur of a stream . . . and religious robes no more spiritual than work clothes."*

Perhaps you have wished you could spend some time in a Tibetan or Benedictine monastery, or perhaps live temporarily as a nun in a cloistered Carmelite convent. There's a way to do this without emigrating from your present life and work. The only traveling you must do is to migrate from your present mind-set about where and who you are.

To enjoy secluded holy places, it is not necessary to retreat. Rather, you must advance into that state of awareness of which Jesus spoke: "The reign of God is here, among you" (see Mark 1: 15). The next time you ponder the possibility of making a retreat, consider instead making an advance.

If you have ever longed to become a monk or nun, try it out. Consider each morning putting on your everyday clothes as a religious habit and treating your home and workplace as your monastery.

In tomorrow's space colonies there will likely be no room for monasteries, convents, ashrams or lamaseries. Perhaps there will be no need for them either.

133

The Holy Eraser Psalm
➤➤➤ ❰❰❰

O Holy One who is everywhere,
      make me a holy eraser
removing the old dividing lines
      of sacred and secular.
For blessed are those who erase
      the artificial boundaries that divide life.

Correct my biased bifocal vision,
      seeing the holy as separate,
as set apart from the temporal world,
      from the fabric of daily life.
For blessed are the eyes
      that see all as good and holy
and fully saturated with you.

Daily empowered as your holy eraser,
      may I boldly wipe out
all of religion's confining graffiti,
      those sharp sanctuary lines
that make the spiritual and practical
      as different as earth is from sea.

Reflection: *This prayer could well be called the Catacomb Psalm, for you are advised never to pray it aloud in public. As the early Christians gathered to pray in catacombs, the underground burial caves of Rome, you may want to go down into your basement to pray this prayer. While religion teaches that God is everywhere, it also has an ageless tradition of painting God-zone lines, borders that separate the holy from the everyday world, all across the Earth.*

The faithful of each religion generally give wholehearted support to this defacing of creation fostered by their own religious denominations. Such boundary lines create a manageable gravity field of religion, conveniently keeping the Holy One out of our daily lives. Yet those who honor the mystical traditions of Taoism, Zen, Sufism, Christianity and Judaism strive to live daily in an Earth cleansed of set-apart sacred spaces.

134

The Holy Family Psalm
→»·«←

In the name of the Father
and the Son
and all the Holy Family.

Holy Spirit of Unity, maker of family,
open my eyes to how wondrously large
is the holy family to which I belong.
Was I a kidnapped child
who grew up thinking
that I belonged to another family?

O Spirit of fiery tongues,

inspire my tongue
so I can enjoy a family homecoming
    as I daily greet all I meet.
Good morning:
    Brother Tree and Sister Bird,
    Brother Dog and Sister Cat,
    Brother Sun and Sister Moon.
Good day and good night:
    Brothers, sisters, cousins all.

With Brother Francis of Assisi,
    with Sufi saints of Islam,
Hindu hermits and Shinto priests,
    I begin my day
    in the name
        of the Father
        and of the Son
        and all the Holy Family.

Reflection: *Islam teaches, "All creatures are the family of God . . . and the most beloved of God are the ones who do the most good to their family." The Japanese religion of Shintoism admonishes, "Do not forget that the world is one great family." In his famous* **Canticle of the Sun**, *Francis of Assisi echoed this global abiding truth.*

Be patient — and a little playful — as you read this psalm, and let your tongue teach you to come home to your family. Even if you're not presently comfortable with it, practice greeting all creatures — even plants, rocks and other seemingly inanimate members of your holy family. Once habit has a hold of your tongue, you may discover eye- and heart-opening mystical experiences.

Since prehistoric times, emigrants have been accompanied by dogs, cats, birds and other animals. Nor, surely, will outer space be petless. A leap out of gravity is involved in seeing and treating

animals not only as pets or even friends, but as brothers and sisters.
Like religious superiority that limits who might be seen as a saved
or chosen people, so too an exclusively human-centered vision is a
sinful discrimination against the holy family of God.

135

Psalm of the Eternal Holy Name
❧≫≪❧

Eternal One, grant me the ears of a mystic
to hear you praying the prayer
of your forever name:

> "I Am,"
> with you,
> in you,
> for you.

> "I Am Who Am,"
> in love with you,
> your lover,
> your guide,
> your freedom,
> your joy,
> your bread,
> your sorrow,
> your death,
> your life,
> your beginning,
> and your end:
>> I AM.

Reflection: *When Moses asked the name of the fiery voice speaking from the burning bush, he was told, "I Am Who Am." The All Holy One went on to say, "This is my name forever; this is my title for all generations." These words of God spoken in Exodus (3: 14-15) are full of powerful implications.*

This prayer-psalm unites us with the "I Am" who was liberation from slavery, the promise of salvation, the covenant maker and the lawgiver of the chosen people of the Torah. Inspired by the Jewish tradition, we pray not to a God who once was or to a God who someday will be, but to a God who is perpetually present as "I Am." In a Holy One with such a self-given name, all clocks and calendars vanish and all generations dissolve into one.

It is strange that the Holy One's preferred name from Exodus — especially since the statement was made with such intensity — is rarely used to address God. Perhaps you can begin to do so in your prayer.

136

The Psalm of Heaven
⋙⋘

Heaven is not up beyond the skies,
    far distant from planet Earth,
a million miles away from us;
    God's home is no faraway heaven.

Probing space with robot-ships
    and farseeing telescopes,
even humans in soaring spacecraft
    have not found God in the heavens.

Look not for God in the heavens,
 for heaven, earth and space
are all within our God,
 and God is forever everywhere.

To find God, simply open your eyes;
 to go to heaven, die not,
but only plunge deeply down inside
 everything and everyone.

 Reflection: *The sixteenth century German Lutheran mystic, Jakob Boehme, answered the twentieth century claim of Russian cosmonauts who said they had gone to the heavens and had not found God. Boehme wrote in* **The Way to Christ***, "If man's eyes were but opened, he should see God everywhere in his heaven; for heaven stands in the innermost, moving everywhere." A verse in the* **Koran** *also expresses this wonderful yet hidden reality: "Wherever you turn, there is the face of God" (***Koran***, Sura II, 115). Practice seeing the face of God wherever you look and you will be delighted and amazed at the consequences.*

137

Psalm of the Dawn of Darkness
➳➳⋘⋘

In space the sun does not really rise; rather,
 it breaks open the dark in splashing splendor.
Awesomely beautiful rises our Earth
 over the rim of the moon,

as stunning and spectacular as a sunrise
    cresting the rim of the Grand Canyon.

The darkness of space is frozen love,
    for Divine Love created dark night before day.
Yet, because the dark has been defaced as evil,
    I need the stillness of silent prayer
to unmask the darkness and thus find you, my God.

O Holy Maker of Darkness and Light,
    wrap me in a prayerful stillness
    whenever evil eclipses my world.
Gathered up in your boundless love,
    I can become your sunrise in the darkness.

Reflection: *The late seventeenth century English Protestant mystic, George Fox, who founded the Society of Friends, the Quakers, taught the power of silent sitting. Coming directly from a mystical experience in which he had been taken up in the Spirit as God made all things new, he made his way to visit a prison. Like all seventeenth century English prisons, it was a terrible place, in which the insane, criminals and all sorts of social outcasts — including religious rebels — were crowded together as if cast into a dark pit.*

Along the way, God spoke to him, "My love was always to thee, and thou art in my love." Fox was encouraged and strengthened by this message, but upon entering the prison was overcome by the great power of darkness. Fox said that, at that moment, he sat still, "having my spirit gathered into the love of God."

The next time you are enjoying living in the light and suddenly darkness dawns in your world with a frightening specter of evil, find a way to be centered in stillness. Gather your scattered self into the love of God, even if you are not able to sit still with eyes closed in prayer. For even in the heart of darkness can be found the zero gravity of God.

138

Psalm of the Sweet Grandeur of God

⋙⋘

O Creative Spirit of Beauty,
  who in creation mirrored
the face of God on Earth
  and in all the heavens,
lift me in my prayer up above
  the flatness of earth
to better see God's grandeur
  in all of holy creation.

Grant me the sweet vision
  of those who truly see
what I only dully look upon,
  so my eyes can taste
in the rich blue of the sky,
  the mellow yellow of the sun
and the sweet silver of the stars,
  the many flavors of God.

Reflection: *The American Calvinist preacher and mystic, Jonathan Edwards, was ordained in 1727 at the Congregational Church in Northampton, Massachusetts, and died in 1758. His mystical experiences gave him new eyes with which to see his world. In his personal account of his life he wrote, ". . . my sense of divine things gradually increased . . . and had more of that inward sweetness. The appearance of everything was altered, there seemed to be, as it were, a calm, sweet cast, or appearance of divine glory, in almost everything."*

While such vision is always a gift from God, we can cultivate the capacity to see the sweetness in the world around us by taking

*time to see with more than eyes. Opening our eyes requires not
just looking, but taking time to see. Today, the word sweetness
has a pious sound, but it can be an apt descriptive word for those
who are able to alter their viewing position. Those who have traveled
out into space are universal in their reports of how beautiful, how
sweet, is Earth when viewed from afar. Consider, then, altering
your perspective, not by traveling into space but by growing new
eyes. Do what Jesus proposed: "Let those with eyes see," to which
we might add, "and taste."*

139

Litany Psalm of All the Saints of God

Blessed are all you holy ones, the saints,
    you who have done the will of God,
and now rejoice in the reward of eternal joy.

Holy men and women who worshiped the All Holy One
    as Rama, Vishnu or the Lord Krishna,
forest hermits, ascetics and wise ones
    whose lives were incarnations of the holy books
    — the Vedas, Upanishads and Gita —
all you Hindu saints, we praise you, for holy are you.

Monks, nuns and all holy followers of the blessed Buddha,
    who, in the peace of Zen, created peace in others,
all who sought the bliss of Nirvana with dedication
    and practiced justice and compassion toward all,
all you Buddhist saints, we praise you, for holy are you.

Chosen people of God, children of Abraham and Sara,

saints Moses and Jacob, Ruth and Rebecca,
holy prophets Isaiah and Jeremiah, and all prophets,
    all you martyrs of Dachau and Buchenwald,
all you Jewish saints, we praise you, for holy are you.

Saints Confucius, Lao Tzu and Chuang Tzu of China,
    all holy men and women of the Orient,
you who lived lives balancing the yin and the yang,
    and all who found wisdom and grace in the Tao,
all you Chinese saints, we praise you, for holy are you.

Holy prophet Mohammed and all holy saints of Islam,
    all who surrendered to the will of Allah,
holy martyrs of Islam, who with your lives
    declared that Allah is One and only One,
all you whirling dervishes and mystic Sufis,
    you ecstatic lovers of the Divine Beloved,
all you saints of the Koran, we praise you, for holy are you.

All you Incas of Peru, holy Mayans and Aztecs of Mexico,
    all you Native children of the sun and stars,
you who with creative love and sacrifice
    raised up wondrous temples to your God,
holy followers of Lord Khonvum, God of the Pygmies,
    holy ones of Tane, God of the Polynesians,
all you saints of all tribes, we praise you, for holy are you.

Saints of the Iroquois, Delaware, Dakotas, Hopi and Sioux,
    holy ones of the Cheyenne, Navajo and Pawnee,
medicine men and women, visionaries and healers,
    all to whom the animals, fish and trees spoke,
all you Native saints, we praise you, for holy are you.

All saints of the Lord Jesus Christ and the Gospel,
    holy husbands and wives, nuns and monks,
    clergy and missionaries and people of God,
all you who lived Gospel lives serving others,
    caring for the poor, the abandoned and the sick,

all you great reformers, preachers and teachers,
    all you holy hermits and mystics,
all you Christian saints, we praise you, for holy are you.

Saints tree, flower, bird and beast, fish and bug,
    saints cat and dog, squirrel and hawk,
sun and moon, stars and clouds, all of creation,
    who perpetually do the will of God
    by living fully who God made you to be,
all saints of creation, we praise you, for holy are you.

All you saints in heaven, we praise you;
    all you saints on earth, we praise you.
All you canonized and uncanonized saints, we praise you;
    all you struggling to be saints, we praise you.
All who are unaware that you are saints, we praise you;
    blessed be all you inside-out saints
    who are presently sinners.
And blessed are all you
    who believe in the Communion of Saints.

 Reflection: *If the first of November's feast of All Saints or All Hallows is celebrated in the future on some distant space station, it should be as encompassingly global as Earth's emigrants living in space. If we are to live prayerfully in that soon-to-arrive tomorrow, in a full human communion with the entire body of God, then we must begin today to pray in a wholly encompassing way.*

Among the most ancient and beautiful prayers of Christianity is the Litany of Saints — prayed not only on the feast of All Saints but at other significant feasts and celebrations as well. The above litany sings of the holiness of all of God's saints. As the title of All Saints suggests, inclusive praise is fitting toward all of God's holy ones.

II. Psalms of Adoration

Adoration is dwarfing prayer
Adoration is shrinking prayer
Adoration is humble prayer
Adoration is undemocratic prayer
Adoration is inequality prayer

In an age of technological wonders the prayer of adoration is an endangered prayer. Yet adoration is a natural prayer response when we contemplate the vast expanses between the stars, even between our sun-star and her closest sister, Alpha Centauri.

This space between our sun-star and her nearest neighbor is out of reach for our minds. So vast are the distances in outer space that they must be measured in light years, and light travels at 670 million miles per hour! To travel to Alpha Centauri would take 4.3 light years; at the speed of NASA's Apollo moon spacecraft such a journey would take 850,000 years. Wonder, which is the womb of the prayer of adoration, follows on the heels of such an awareness, and that's only to our next-door star!

The following psalm-prayers are space station songs of adoration for those still bound to planet Earth yet eager to open the womb of wonder.

140

Adoration of the Blessed Sacrament Psalm
⇒≫‹‹⇐

Round, blue and brown world,
    holy, holy are you.
Arms of whirling white clouds

embracing this sacred Earth,
like white wings of the holy;
holy, holy are you.

I believe! Help my unbelief;
like those swirling clouds,
I long to fully embrace
this first blessed sacrament,
for saturated with the sacred
are your soil, sky and seas.

O my soul, remove your sandals
for all Earth is holy land,
consecrated by God's words
spoken in the beginning,
when Earth was still naked
of all religious sanctuaries.

Reflection: *The first sacrament created by God was creation — an outward physical sign of the invisible divine love, invested with the living presence of the Divine Creator.*

Roman Catholicism in the Middle Ages created a ritual for adoring Jesus Christ present in the consecrated host. Many are the ways to adore the presence of Christ in our midst. One way was mentioned in the introduction to this section: To view Earth from space or to prayerfully contemplate a photograph of Earth taken from space is an invitation to practice the prayer of awe.

*Adoration is a necessary human prayer, and every healthy spiritual life should include adoration. We have a human need to prostrate ourselves on the ground before that which is awesome, what is filled with wonder and is totally other than us. Such prayer is literally to pray before, from the Latin, **ad-orare**.*

As many as the stars are the ways we can prostrate ourselves in adoration. Rather than fearing that you might be considered a pagan if you adore God in the first sacrament, creation, fear that even though you have eyes you may be blind to the wonder of God.

141

The Coffee Cup Adoration Psalm

Wondrous God, I can get drunk,
    dizzy with devotion,
drinking from my coffee cup
    as I peer inside its round rim
and imagine our entire solar system,
    the sun and her nine far-flung planets,
swirling around in the sea of warm brown coffee.

When I use the magic of imagination,
    and shrink our giant solar system
so it fits inside my coffee cup,
    I'm overwhelmed with awe
that our vast Milky Way galaxy
    would then spiral out
as large as all of North America.

O Creator God of awesome wonders,
    at the mere thought of our galaxy,
480 million billion miles wide,
    I bow down in adoration:
Holy, holy and wondrous are you;
    your glory extends so far beyond
the 100 billion such galaxies
    you've sprinkled like salt
over this the black tablecloth
    of our known universe.

Reflection: *Imagination is the suitcase offered to gypsy-emigrants who are forced to stay at home on this planet. Spooning your morning coffee with imagination is a way of traveling beyond the threshold of your small mind.*

The Hebrew word for heaven is plural: the term heavens implies all that exists out there in space. For heaven's sake, don't overlook the heavens if you wish to pray the prayer of adoration. Marvel as you watch your coffee or tea swirl like the solar system as you consider how very minuscule you are in comparison. Marvel and then sing out in wonder that you are as important to God, as much loved, as any solar system.

142

The Milky Way Galaxy Psalm
⇒⇒ ⇐⇐

Look up at the night sky, Abraham was told,
    and contemplate the vast expanse of stars.
Look up at the night sky, children of Abraham,
    and adore before the sacrament of the stars.
Look up at the Milky Way, winding its white way,
    starry eyed by the billions across a night sky.
Be in awe that this is no lazy lane of lights
    but a cosmic circus-carousel spiral galaxy
that every 230 million years turns round once.

In open-mouthed awe I pray in wonderment, O God,
    for your whirling dervish dancer of a galaxy
has only circled twenty times since our sun's birth,
    only ten times since oxygen was invented,
moving less than one hundredth of a turn
    since ancient humans stood up straight.

For me, to look up at this milky way of stars
    is to see the silver stream of stars as Mother's Milk,
and so to gape in a dwarf's prayer, my God,
    for the heavens are immeasurably full of your glory.

Reflection: *Saintly sterile Abraham was called to look up and see the night sky as a sparkling promise of his heritage of countless sons and daughters — and so to marvel. As sterile as Sara and Abraham were prior to God's blessing, be that fruitful as you look up at the night sky's spiral galaxy flowing across the horizon like a stream of spilled milk. Be fertile in your adoration, your gaping-in-humble-wonder prayer as you contemplate what is just one out of the over 100 billion presently known galaxies in the universe.*

No cathedral or mosque ever had a more awe-inspiring mosaic dome than God's night sky star temple. Go out and visit that temple frequently to keep your balance in life. However, note this caution: Keeping your balance may require losing it and falling on your knees in the zero gravity of adoration.

143

Psalm of Our Addictive God
❧❧❧❦❦❦

Yes, I fear it's true, Most Holy God,
    that creating is addictive for you.
Oh, after your six days of laboring,
    you rested on the seventh day
and stepped back to admire your work,
    smiling with satisfaction.

But there is no rest for the holy,
    and on Monday for millenniums on end
you returned to create with great delight
    brand new suns and moons.
As weeks of creation followed,

you birthed billions of planets,
and trillions of new young stars.

With our telescope eyes firmly pressed
to the cosmic nursery window,
we, your children, gape in holy awe,
watching stars being born in clusters
in your endless inventive laboratory,
the Eden of eternal creativity.

Blessed are these new telescope eyes
which see that you are not only love,
but never-ending, ever-fresh love,
an Ageless Artist addicted to creating.

O blessedly exciting, infinitely expanding God,
blessed are we to be created in your image,
blessed that you are not stale and static,
resting in an eternal remote-control retirement
after your wondrous Genesis creation days.

Reflection: *Genesis began a merry-go-round of perpetual creation that should excite our hearts to wonder and adoration that the All Holy One seems never to tire of creating.*

Made in God's image, we need to ask God to kiss awake the sleeping beauty of the holy gift of imagination and creativity. This gift has fallen under the curse of the evil witch of our assembly-line, mass-produced, cookie-cutter contemporary society. Kiss your slumbering divine gift with love to awaken it today with the knowledge that the Holy Creative One is eager for you to bring your gift and come out and play!

The prayer of adoration is more than falling facedown to the earth in wonder. It also calls us to a-door, as in opening a door. It calls us to open the doors of our personal gifts, the doors to wondrous worlds of beauty hidden within ourselves.

144

The Lunar Lover Psalm

Sister of the yellow sphere,
    O night white orb of lovers,
  Earth's one and only moon,
gravity gripper of ocean tides and weak minds,
    whose birthday was on Genesis day four,
prayerfully pull me down into adoration.

If 100 billion planets spin around their suns
    in just our one small galaxy,
and some planets are blessed with several moons,
    then, O Ever-Generous, Abundantly Creative Lover,
there may be more than a trillion lovers' moons
    gravitating out there in space!
The thought of so many Passover, harvest and blue moons,
    fills me, one of your lunatic lovers, with great wonder.

Holy One, too generous to make only one moon,
    you couldn't restrain your creative urge.
So you repeated Genesis day four a billion times
    to birth moons upon moons to the millions.
Your wild imagination could not stop at one Earth,
    so you dreamed up more than 100 billion planets.
Your appetite to create galaxies was so great
    that you likewise poured out some 100 billion.

May adoration bring me prayerfully to my knees
    that some day soon our telescope eyes,
having grown large enough, will be able to see
    that one universe was not enough either.
Holy, holy and wholly unfathomable are you,
    my Ever-Expanding, Eternal Holy Mystery.

Reflection: *Moon-watching was a favorite activity among contemplative Orientals, who developed marvelous rituals for watching the moon rise from their teahouses. Moon-watching soothes the soul. But it is also made for lovers, especially lunatic lovers of the Holy Creator, who couldn't stop making moons because they were so beautiful.*

Consider setting aside an adoration night, a prayer time for going outside when a full moon is rising. As you watch the great white orb ascending in its poetic beauty, imagine the sky moon-jammed with billions if not trillions of these mystical moons. Then give thanks for our one beautiful, visible moon as you fill your gaze and your soul with wonder.

145

The Sun Psalm*

⟶⟫ ⟪⟵

O glorious sun, whom ancients worshipped
    as the holy source of light and life,
I do not adore you, yet I'm in awe of you,
    for your daytime sunny presence is everywhere
except when you're temporarily hidden from view
    by a passing parade of dull, gray clouds.

Great daystar, our luminous gift from God,
    you not only nourish life and fire up my spirit,
    you are my mentor in the sky:
As I shade my eyes from your blazing light,
    I learn in that prayerful gaze
my vocation to be the light of the world.

Sky furnace, holy hydrogen cosmic candle,

I marvel at your ongoing martyrs' death.
For every second of every day you consume
　　four and half millions tons of yourself
to be light, warmth and life for the world.

Inspire me, sun sacrament in the sky
　　to also consume myself in a sacred sacrificial fire,
　　to be light and life for the world around me.
Wherever I go, may dark shadows of despair
　　retreat before my sunny humor and warm love,
and may seeds sprout and life abound in my path.

Reflection: *This psalm sings of the glory of the sun as a reflection of the Son. For the sun is a sacrament of the self-consuming fire of being the light, warmth and life of our world. For the ancients in the Near East, the sacred sign of the sun was *, the asterisk. In Greek the name means "little sun." While at one time the mark of the asterisk had a special significance, it is usually used today simply as a reference mark.*

When you are noting in your schedule an appointment to perform some task that will call for sacrifice, consider making an * behind it. Use it as a secret sign to encourage you to be like the sun, to consume yourself in the process of being light and life for others.

It has been a tradition for Catholic bishops to place a +, a cross, before their official signatures. Consider making an * before your name, a symbol of which perhaps only you will know the meaning. As you write down your *, pray a brief prayer to be sun-like, to be the light of the world, in all you do.

III. The End Psalms

This book of prayers, like any other book, has an ending, just as worlds, stars, millenniums and movements all have their endings. Only God is without end, and God is the Beloved Endlessly Awesome One to whom these psalms are addressed. While we may fear our final endings, by the boundless generosity of God we also share in eternity, forever without end when we are fully alive in the Divine Mystery.

146

The End of the World Psalm: A Song of Our Sun-Star's Armageddon Sunset

"The sun will be forever darkened,
    the moon will not shed its pale light,
and the stars will fall from the sky
    on that day of great tribulation."

Woe to this world in those dark times
    when the sun will be entirely extinguished —
but not before our dying star bloats
    to a hundred times its present size,
swelling beyond our planet's orbit,
    melting continents like cheese,
boiling seas and vaporizing the Earth.

A death a million years long

will be our dying sun's bloating agony,
as it collapses in upon itself
in spasms of cosmic coughing,
shrinking to the size of planet Earth;
finally, the fading sun-star will shrink
to only sixteen tons of lifeless cooling matter,
and quietly, unnoticed, will die.

Then, like an old cowboy rolling up a cigarette
out on the range under a starry sky,
a grinning God will roll up another sun,
and light it with the snap of a supernova.

 Reflection: *The end of this book brings us to the End, a deliciously favorite subject for prophets of all persuasions. Yet the world ends daily in almost every conceivable way, from divorce and death to bankruptcy and broken hearts, so be prepared.*

With his telescopic eye, Jesus predicted the end of the world. Unfortunately, the clock of many of his followers wasn't working correctly. His prediction was correct, only the purported timing was off. Not in Jesus' generation, not a thousand years or two thousand later, was the sun to be darkened and the stars fall from the skies, but perhaps in another five or six billion years.

Six billion years from now? No need to repent or swear never to sin again. No need to give away all your possessions or dress up in your Easter Apocalyptic clothes to await the End. Our middle-aged sun is in good health, and barring any unforeseen accidents will continue to be the light of the world for a long time.

Astronomers, applying the chilly stethoscope of astrophysics, have also predicted the distant death of the sun, which means the end of our world as well. In her old age our daystar will use up her cellar of hydrogen as she gasps for life; she will burn helium and then bloat to one hundred times her middle-aged body size, engulfing planet Earth in a raging giant of a fireball, before imploding and becoming a dead cinder in space.

Who will notice, or even care, if one old-aging sun-star dies? Who will miss one star among the one or two hundred billion in our galaxy alone, not to mention those in the one hundred billion other galaxies in the universe?

God will.

147

The New Millennium Psalm
⋙ ⋘

God of no time, O Timeless One,
    open wide our hearts to perceive
each minute as a new millennium,
    a point of time that begins
a calendar of new birth beginnings
    and dates the death endings of the old.

Awaken us, O God, to how each day
    is the dawn of a new millennium
for some plant, creature, planet or star
    in your ever-expanding universe,
billions of years old yet ever-youthening,
    whose cosmic calendar began time.

O Divine One, you who are before time,
    may we who live on this planet of countless calendars
creatively celebrate a new millennium of our calendar
    so as to learn how to welcome with joyful wonder
each new millennium moment of Life.

Reflection: *Planet Earth has birthed a collection of calendars: Jewish, Roman, Greek, Christian, Islamic, Byzantine, Hindu, Chinese and Japanese, along with the chronological records of every culture and clan. The ancient Egyptians and Mayans considered calendar-making a sacred, priestly act; theirs and other ancient calendars continue to count years and millenniums even to this day.*

The present Christian calendar of the Western secular world counts time from the date of the birth of Jesus the Christ. Let the arrival of the second millennium of that most significant event be celebrated with humility and reverence for the planet's older calendars and those who honor them. Regardless of which calendar any of us follow today, may each present moment be celebrated as the eternal still point of sacred time.

148

The Last Psalm
-=>> <<=-

Hallelujah!
    Praise God everywhere
  on Earth and in space.
All creation wildly applaud
  the Almighty One.
Praise God to the outermost edges of the universe
  and beyond.
Praise God, all you supernovas and supermarkets,
    all you mosques and marketplaces,
    all you cathedrals and cabarets,
    all you temples and tennis courts.

Alleluia!
Praise God with resounding cymbals,
    and with crashing markets.
Praise God, you powerful majestic pipe organs
    and you New Orleans jazz bands.
Praise God, you circus carousel calliopes,
    and all you castanet-clicking gypsy caravans.
Praise God, all you with dancing feet,
    and all you with walkers and canes.

Hallelujah!
Praise our Great God of Ten Thousand Names.
    Praise God, all you holy saints in heaven.
Praise God, all you haloless saints on Earth.

Let everything that lives on the Earth
    and in the oceans and seas,
    and in the sea of space,
    praise the Life that is
    and was and shall ever be.
        Alleluia!
        Alleluia!
        Alleluia!

Bibliography and Resources

APPLEBAUM, DAVID, "Arcs." *Parabola*, Fall 1997.

BAMFORD, CHRISTOPHER, "Culture of the Heart." *Parabola*, Winter 1995.

BANKS, COLEMAN, *The Illuminated Rumi*. Broadway Books, New York, 1997.

BERGANT, DIANNE, and KARRIS, ROBERT, *The Collegeville Bible Commentary*. The Liturgical Press, Collegeville, Minn., 1989.

BLY, ROBERT, *The Kabir Book*. Beacon Press, Boston, 1971.

BOORSTIN, DANIEL, *The Creators*. Vintage Books, New York, 1992.

BUECHNER, FREDERICK, *On the Road with the Archangel*. Harper, San Francisco, 1997.

BURHOLT, S. PAUL, "Sacred Threshold." *Parabola*, Spring 1998.

CALDECOTT, STRATFORD, "I Thirst to Be Thirsted For." *Parabola*, Winter 1995.

EVANS, IVOR, *Brewer's Dictionary of Phrase & Fable*. Harper & Row, New York, 1981.

FREMANTLE, ANNE, *The Protestant Mystics*. New American Library, New York, 1965.

GELINEAU, JOSEPH, *The Psalms*. The Grail, London, 1963.

GREEN, ARTHUR, and HOLTZ, BARRY, *Your Word is Fire: The Hasidic Masters on Contemplative Prayer*. Paulist Press, New York, 1977.

HAMILL, SAM, "The Erotic Spirit." *Parabola*, Winter 1995.

MCALEER, NEIL, *The Cosmic Mind-Boggling Book*. Warner Books, 1982.

MCKENZIE, JOHN, *Dictionary of the Bible*. Bruce Publishing Co., Milwaukee, 1965.

MOSES, JEFFREY, *Oneness: Great Principles Shared by All Religions.* Fawcett Columbine, New York, 1989.

RAMANUJAN, A.K., *Speaking of Siva.* Penguin Books, Baltimore, 1973.

ROTHENBERG, DAVID, "Sound Traces." *Parabola*, Summer 1997.

ROSENZWEIG, FRANZ, "The Love of God, the Love of Man." *Parabola*, Winter 1995.

SAGAN, CARL, *Cosmos.* Random House, New York, 1980.

SCHAEFFER, PAMELA, "Medieval Manuscripts Upend Assumptions." *National Catholic Reporter*, January 9, 1998.

WALKER, BRIAN, *Hua Hu Ching: The Unknown Teachings of Lao Tzu.* Harper, San Francisco, 1992.

WILSON, A.N., *Paul: The Mind of the Apostle.* W.W. Norton & Company, New York, 1997.

WINTER, ART, "Spirit's 'Giddyap' Won't Move Dead Horses." *National Catholic Reporter*, December 12, 1997.

ZALESKI, IRMA, "Treasure Within." *Parabola*, Fall 1997.

Index Guide to Prayer Themes

*The prayer themes below are addressed in this book's psalms as well as their accompanying reflections. Each theme listed in bold type is part of a psalm's title. All the numerical references below refer to **psalm numbers**, not page numbers.*

The Author
Edward M. Hays

Many authors have used a middle initial to distinguish themselves from authors with the same name. Their readers usually do not know the name indicated by that initial. Edward Hays says that even many of his close friends do not know what his middle initial stands for. Whenever asked about it, he jokingly tells people that the "M" is for "Mercury," since his parents wanted a car. He adds that it would have been a fitting middle name since Mercury was a Roman god who was the messenger of the gods. Authors, Hays says, often have that responsibility, even if they don't wear Mercury's winged hat, winged sandals or carry a caduceus. He further suggests that it would have been an appropriate name for him because Mercury was also the patron god of rogues and vagabonds and because *mercurial* means to be lighthearted and unpredictable — which Hays also strives to be.

Although in his childhood years he found his actual middle name embarrassing and never revealed it to his school mates, now in his later years he takes delight in having the ancient Roman name of Marcellus. He was given his middle name at Baptism, in honor of his maternal grandfather, and so bears it today with both pleasure and pride.

At age eighteen, E. Marcellus Hays was left in a basket on the doorstep of the Benedictine Monastery of Conception Abbey at Conception, Missouri. The kindly monks took him in and gave him his college liberal arts and theological education. The monks also instilled in him a great devotion for the Psalms of David, which were the core of their prayer. The Psalms became his daily prayer throughout his eight years of study at the Abbey, and beyond.

Edward Marcellus was ordained a priest for the Archdiocese of Kansas City in Kansas in 1958. He served in parish ministry for thirteen years, seven of which were with the Pottawatomie Native American tribe at Mayetta, Kansas. After an extended prayer pilgrimage to the Near East and India, he served from 1972 to 1995 as the director of a lay contemplative prayer community at the Archdiocesan House of Prayer, Shantivanam. The author of twenty-one books on prayer and contemporary spirituality and a self-taught artist, he presently serves as the priest chaplain to the Kansas State Penitentiary located in Lansing, Kansas.